WILLIAM
MORRIS

CHANCELLOR PRESS

HELEN DORE

WILLIAM MORRIS

For Geoffrey, Mary and Richard

Above: Kelmscott Manor, watercolour by May Morris

Overleaf: Original design for Windrush cotton

Endpapers: Acorn wallpaper, 1880

First published in 1996 by Hamlyn

This edition published in 2003 by Chancellor Press, an imprint of
Bounty Books, a division of Octopus Publishing Group Ltd,
2-4 Heron Quays, London E14 4JP

Copyright © Reed International Books Ltd 1990

ISBN 0 7537 0709 8

Produced by Toppan Printing Co. (H.K.) Ltd
Printed and bound in China

CONTENTS

William Morris, portrait by W.B. Richmond

INTRODUCTION

William Morris's career was marked by an extraordinary breadth of interest and range of achievement, as a poet and writer of romance, scholar and critic, ardent socialist and above all as a designer. His intense love of the decorative arts was founded on his belief in the strength of the medieval ideal of craftsmanship, in which the designer and workman were one. Morris brought his artistic convictions to bear on his own working life, being skilled in all the arts to which he contributed so much, and elevating the concept of design above the mass-production of the Victorian era, while remaining eminently practical and down to earth in his approach.

When William Morris died in 1896, at the age of 62, the output of his working life had been prodigious by any standards. Today he is best remembered for his remarkable achievements in the decorative arts, and this book is concerned exclusively with his work as a designer in a great variety of media, including stained glass, hand-painted tiles, tapestries and other woven textiles, embroideries, rugs and carpets, as well as the exquisite and well-loved hand-printed wallpapers and chintzes with which he transformed the cluttered interiors of many Victorian homes, becoming a household word for good taste in his own time.

However, William Morris was not just an outstanding designer, who towards the end of his life even added type design and fine printing to the already extraordinary range of his artistic activities. He was also a distinguished scholar, linguist and translator, and later in life a committed socialist, actively participating in the early Labour Movement and in building the emerging Socialist Party; he helped found the Socialist League in 1884 and remained closely involved with its activities until his resignation in 1890. His artistic ideals were always closely related to his social concerns, based on his conviction that the enjoyment of art, far from being esoteric or rarefied, was part of man's birthright and as such part of everyday life: he was the author of many eloquent essays and articles on the arts and socialism.

As his reputation grew he established himself as a very popular guest speaker — five of the most important of his lectures on the arts and related matters were published under the title *Hopes and Fears for Art*, and his collected writings run to 24 volumes. Furthermore, in his own day Morris was especially well known as a poet, and particularly as the author of the enormously successful *Earthly Paradise*.

Morris literally believed all he lived in, and sincerity and single-mindedness were just two of his many remarkable qualities. His great friend and fellow artist, Edward Burne-Jones, well summed up the consistency of Morris's life's work when he described his life as 'one continuous course', going on to add: 'His earliest enthusiasms were his latest'. Enthusiasm was another of Morris's outstanding characteristics: despite his very full life, he was always a prolific correspondent, and his letters, many of which read like diary entries, often describe a scene or experience which had impressed him, or some quite technical aspect of his work currently in hand, in enthusiastic, vivid detail, which makes irresistible and compelling reading. Morris's voice can be clearly heard in his correspondence, and indeed in everything he wrote. His letters, together with the recollections of those who knew him, particularly those of his beloved younger daughter

May, of his secretary Sidney Cockerell in his Boswell-like diaries, and of his biographer J. W. Mackail, who published his masterly *Life* in 1899, create a clear image of Morris's abundantly energetic personality.

It was the wide range of his interests, and the way he combined extraordinary intellectual acumen, capacity to absorb information, and breadth of artistic vision with an accessible, down-to-

Far left: Jasmine Trellis/Jasmine Trail printed cotton. William Morris's earliest-known textile design, made in 1868–70

Below: The Morris and Burne-Jones families in the garden of The Grange, Fulham

earth approach which often expressed itself in practical, largely self-taught skills, that made him so outstanding, both as a man and as an artist. One of the qualities which his friends must have found especially endearing was his sense of fun and his ability to enjoy himself. He worked tremendously hard, but had the rare gift of making all he did seem effortless: 'he never seemed to be particularly busy', as Burne-Jones put it.

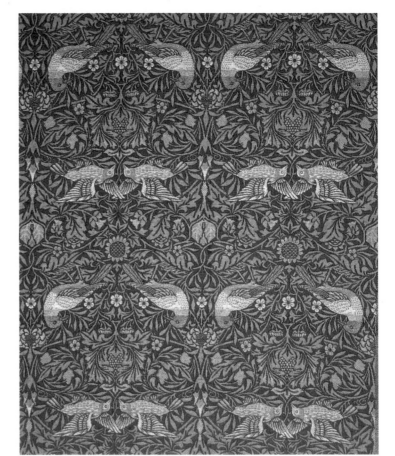

Below: Bird, *woven wool double cloth, 1878. One of Morris's most popular fabrics for curtains and upholstery*

Morris's artistic beliefs

Creative in so many areas, and the master of such a variety of media, Morris could be likened to a kind of Victorian Renaissance man. However, this would be ironic, because for Morris the Renaissance, far from being a cultural flowering, was the root of all evil in modern civilization, paving the way for mechanization and ultimately the slavishly imitative, lifeless and vulgarly philistine art of the Victorian era which he abhorred as much as he did the enslavement of man by the Industrial Revolution. He believed that the Renaissance on the one hand, with its emphasis on classical models, and modern technology on the other, leading inevitably to commercially oriented mass-production, had between them disrupted the natural spontaneous growth of Western art.

For Morris, the only solution was a return to the methods of medieval craftsmanship. Medieval craft values epitomized for him the right approach to the decorative arts, when from original concept to finished product, the work of art remained in the hands of the same craftsman, who was both artist and artisan, unlike the split between design and production which all too often made of the workman a mindless drudge with no understanding of or feel for design. The medieval workman remained the prototype for Morris's concept of the modern craftsman/designer, and he regarded the medieval period as a kind of Golden Age, albeit in a very positive and constructive way. Indeed, the paradox of Morris was that

had an amazing facility for the art of stained glass, and indeed his versatility and extraordinarily instinctive ability were frequently remarked upon by his contemporaries. He researched the technique of vegetable dyeing and worked in the vats discovering how to produce natural, as opposed to chemically reproduced, colours, undoubtedly one of the key secrets to his success as a pattern designer of chintzes. He was also a remarkable calligrapher and illuminator, and designer of two distinctive typefaces. He did all his own designing, or worked in collaboration with the close circle of trusted artist friends who formed the backbone of his business enterprise. Believing as he did that the designer and workman should ideally be one, it was never his practice to employ professional designers, who he felt all too often had no understand-

ing of how their designs would be executed, with inevitably hackneyed, repetitive results.

This must largely account for the freshness that is characteristic of all Morris's work, and one of its most endearing and enduring qualities. Many of Morris's finest designs were based on close observation of nature in the English countryside and gardens, expressing his love of birds, wild flowers and cottage garden plants: 'nothing in the open air escaped him', according to his daughter May. First-hand observation of nature combined admirably in his work with an outstanding ability to make creative use of the art forms of the past which he admired: as he put it during his Examination by the Royal Commissioners on Technical Instruction in 1882 – a most valuable statement of his beliefs as designer and artist/craftsman – a designer 'is bound to study old examples, but he is also bound to

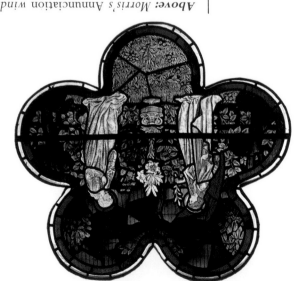

Above: Morris's Annunciation window for All Saints, Middleton Cheney, Northants, 1865

supplement that by a careful study of nature'.

Just as he believed that the medieval craftsman, with his inherited traditional skills and high standards of workman-ship, was able to derive real pleasure from his work — so different from the mindless drudgery of the machine-bound factory worker — and thereby convey the same sense of pleasure to the viewer/user, so he was convinced that art is for everyone and should touch every part of everyday life, however mundane. One of Morris's greatest convictions was that nothing can be a true work of art unless it is useful. His celebrated maxim, 'Have nothing in your houses that you do not know to be useful, or believe to be beautiful' can be universally applied to all his work.

William Morris once expressed the fear that reform in art which is founded on individualism must perish with the individuals who have set it going'. However, this fear was ill-founded, for his art lives on today, internationally recognized and admired, as it had already been within his own time.

Below: Honeysuckle wallpaper, 1883, with left, its original design

Right: Morris's original design for the Columbine/Bluebell chintz, 1876

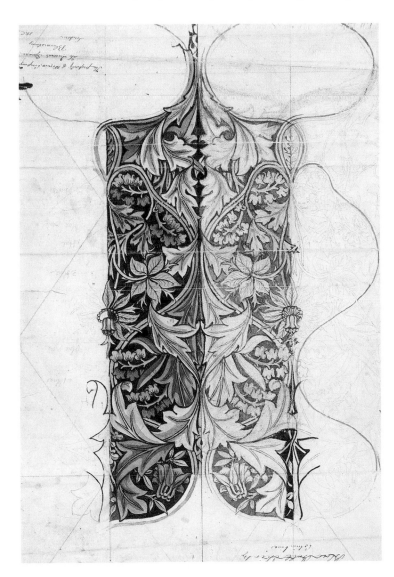

High Street, Oxford. Watercolour by Noel Harry Leaver (1889-1951)

Chapter One

CHILDHOOD AND OXFORD (1834-56)

William Morris's literary and artistic tastes emerged at an early age. He was an avid reader, particularly of tales of chivalry and romance, and architecture and the natural world also became lifelong enthusiasms during childhood. He continued to develop these interests when he went up to Oxford – still essentially a medieval city – in 1853. He was intensely happy during his years there, forming friendships and making artistic and literary discoveries which would be crucial to his subsequent career.

The Morris family was of Welsh descent. William Morris's grandfather had left Wales in the latter part of the 18th century to settle in business in Worcester. His son William married Emma Shelton, from another prosperous Worcester family, at the age of 30, and became a successful broker in London. The couple set up home in Lombard Street, in the City, and it was here that their first two children, Emma and Henrietta, were born.

In 1833 the Morris family moved to Walthamstow, still entirely rural, but already popular as a place of residence for well-to-do City businessmen. William was born here on 24 March 1834.

Below: Drawing by E.H. New of Elm House, Walthamstow, Morris's birthplace

Significantly, in view of his later socialist beliefs, this was the year of the Tolpuddle Martyrs, and the whole of his childhood coincided with the working man's growing struggle against the conditions created by the relentless industrialization which became so abhorrent to William Morris in later life.

William was followed by two more sisters, Isabella and Alice, and four brothers, Hugh, Thomas, Arthur and Edgar, but although William was very close to his sister Emma in childhood, there appears to have been curiously little sustained contact between him and his siblings: only his youngest brother, Edgar, would join him in his work, at Merton Abbey.

The Morris family lived first at Elm House, Clay Hill, overlooking the Lea Valley. This was William's birthplace — the four-poster bed in which he was born can be seen today in Mrs Morris's bedroom at Kelmscott Manor. As the family fortunes prospered, the Morrises moved to Woodford Hall, a Palladian mansion set in 50 acres of grounds on the fringe of Epping Forest; then, after Mr Morris's death in 1849, to Water House, Walthamstow. Since 1950 this fine mid-18th century building has housed the William Morris Gallery, a fascinating permanent collection illustrating the full range of Morris's work and his influence on the Arts and Crafts Movement. Neither of Morris's two other childhood homes is still standing, but there is a charming drawing of Elm House among the illustrations commissioned from E. H. New for J. W. Mackail's biography of Morris.

When William's father died he left his family very well provided for, as the result of successful speculation in copper shares. The 272 shares in a West Country copper mine, which Mr Morris originally bought at £1 a share, soared to an amazing £800 each as a result of increased production to meet the demands of the expanding engineering industry. This capital sum of over £200,000 ensured a comfortable and carefree childhood, undoubtedly a very important factor in William Morris's development. It also provided a substantial annuity when he came of age, and this would enable him to live and work on his own terms, relatively free of money worries, a fact which he himself would be the first to acknowledge. As he put it in an address in 1880 to the School of Science and Art at the Wedgwood Institute, Burslem, in terms which show that he took nothing for granted: 'it was my good luck only of being born respectable and rich, that has put me this side of the window among delightful books and lovely works of art'. It was of course not without irony, and was certainly a source of some embarrassment to Morris, that a life dedicated to the decorative arts, based on a conscious reaction against the mechanization of the Victorian industrial age, should have initially been made possible by finance derived directly from this very industrialization.

Above: Woodford Hall, South Woodford, Essex, Morris's boyhood home from 1840–8

Chivalry and romance

As a child Morris had every opportunity to indulge his literary and artistic tastes which emerged at a remarkably early age. His appetite and facility for reading were unusual, for it seems that he had read all of Scott's Waverley novels by the age of seven. A favourite book was Clara Reeve's Gothic novel, *The Old English Baron*, which he read with his favourite sister Emma, acquiring an early taste for chivalry and romance which would remain with him through-out his life and colour much of his work. This was not confined to books: William was given a miniature toy suit of armour which he wore to act out the part of a medieval knight, riding on his Shetland pony through the glades of Epping Forest, then an idyllic, fairytale place.

He enjoyed visiting Queen Elizabeth I's hunting lodge in the centre of the Forest, and especially loved its dense hornbeam thickets which would often recur in his poetry and prose romances. Later in life Morris became deeply concerned about the wholesale felling of trees in Epping Forest, which always retained a special place in his affections. Epping was certainly the source of his lifelong love of trees, flowers and birds that so often inspired his design patterns: images formed in childhood of flower-strewn fields, the outline of leafy boughs against the sky, and branches heavy with fruit, stayed with him for all of his working life. Like many children before and since, he had his own little garden at home, in which he cultivated the interest in horticul-

ture which would remain with him as an important element in all his adult homes. During childhood, too, he first became acquainted, in his father's library, with Gerard's *Herbal*, which would provide him later in his working career with practical information for experiments with natural dyes as well as inspiration for designs.

As early as the age of eight, Morris showed signs of what would later become a strong and abiding interest in architecture. A visit with his father to Canterbury Cathedral made a powerful impact on him – he later said it was as though the gates of heaven had opened – and over 30 years later, when he was closely involved with the Society for the Protection of Ancient Buildings (which he affectionately called 'Anti-Scrape'), one of the Society's first preoccupations was the restoration of the choir at Canterbury.

Schooldays

In 1848 (doubly significant in terms of Morris's later development, being the year of the foundation of the Pre-Raphaelite Brotherhood and the publication of Marx and Engels's *Communist Manifesto*), William was sent to school at Marlborough College, along with 100 other new boys. The fact that the school had been only recently founded may explain the lax and rough-and-ready

Right: Bachelor's Button wallpaper, 1892. Morris's passion for plants, dating from childhood, remained with him all his life, inspiring many of his designs

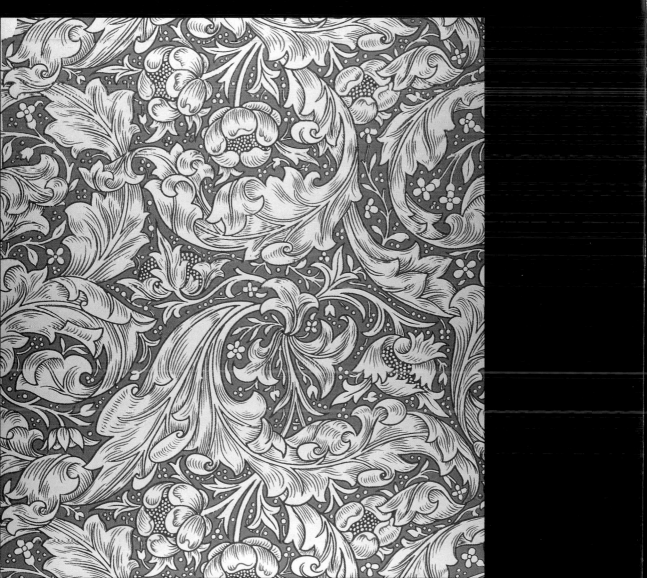

ways William experienced there. He received little formal education, but made good use of the well-stocked library, which was particularly strong in archaeology and ecclesiastical architecture, developing his special interest in these subjects and the ability to absorb information which would later cause an Oxford friend to exclaim: 'How Morris seems to know things, doesn't he!' In fact Marlborough must have contributed indirectly to Morris's extraordinary facility for teaching himself which emerged as such a striking feature of his working life. Also, during his schooldays, he demonstrated his powers of concentration and expertise with his hands in a compulsive love of netting. Just as Epping Forest had been on William's doorstep at home, another enchanted forest – Savernake – with its magnificent ancient oaks, lay invitingly close to Marlborough, and the young

Morris, who was regarded as something of a solitary by his schoolmates, loved to ramble here. His lifelong enthusiasm for ancient monuments was awakened by the round barrows of Silbury Hill and the stone circles of Avebury, Britain's largest megalithic prehistoric monument, which were also sited near Marlborough, and which he described in an excited letter of 13 April 1849 to his sister Emma. This letter also gives a minute description of a water meadow, and the graphic quality of the details with which Morris brings his subject to life is characteristic of the tone he would retain in profuse correspondence throughout his life. His letters are stimulating and informative to read

Above: Elm House, Morris's birthplace, overlooked the river Lea, whose name he gave to this chintz, designed in 1885

Below: *Marlborough College, founded in 1843. Morris was a pupil here for three years from 1848–51*

Oxford

The years Morris spent at Oxford University were crucial, and on his own admission later, the happiest of his life. Most importantly, they were truly formative for him as an artist, in terms of his response to his surroundings, of lifelong friendships formed with kindred spirits, and of the development of his tastes through discussion and reading. Morris went up to Exeter College to study theology, in which he would obtain a pass degree, but in fact he never rated the academic tuition provided by

schoolmaster from Forest School, Walthamstow. Another important chapter in his early development was about to begin.

today, and must have thrilled and absorbed their recipients.

In 1851 an incident occurred which seems significant in the light of the position Morris later adopted as crafts-man/designer. This was the year of the Great Exhibition, the Victorian age's triumphant showcase for its artefacts and technical expertise. But William would have none of it. When a family visit was organized to the Exhibition in Hyde Park, he refused to go in to view exhibits which he described as 'wonder-fully ugly'.

At the end of this year there was a mutiny among the boys at Marlborough – the result of poor management on the part of the people running the school – and Morris's mother, now a widow, decided that he should not return after Christmas. Instead, he remained at home to be privately tutored for the Oxford University entrance examina-tion by the Rev. F. B. Guy, a local

the University very highly; it was the *genius loci* and the opportunities to discover things for himself that were all-important to him as an undergraduate. In the early 1850s Oxford was still very much a medieval city, the beauty of its buildings and their setting as yet unaffected by the vulgar restoration work Morris would lament later in life: in a letter to the *Daily News* of 20 November 1885, for example, written at a time when he was appealing through the Press for the conservation of the City churches, Westminster Abbey, Rouen, Chichester and Peterborough cathedrals, he issued an impassioned plea to spare 'the few specimens of ancient town architecture which they have not yet had time to destroy . . . Oxford thirty years ago, when I first knew it, was full of these treasures'. His description of Oxford as 'a vision of grey-roofed houses and a long winding street, and the sound of many bells',

Below: Some 30 years after going up to Exeter College, Oxford, Morris and Burne-Jones presented the college with their splendid Adoration of the Magi tapestry

whose 'memory has been an abiding influence and pleasure in my life' well conveys the depth of his feeling for the place.

In the entrance examination Morris handed in his Horace paper early, which did not go unnoticed by the candidate sitting next to him. This was Edward Burne-Jones, who became Morris's closest lifelong friend, and in collaboration with whom he would produce some of his most memorable work. Burne-Jones, the son of a Birmingham picture framer, introduced Morris to a number of friends from his home town at Pembroke College: Charles Faulkner, later to become a business partner, R. W. Dixon, who would officiate at Morris's marriage, William Fulford and Cornell (Crom) Price. They spent a lot of time in each other's company, in discussion and reading, and with these friends Morris felt part of a group for the first time, a fact which would be important to the subsequent development of a career in which group as well as solo activity would play a vital part.

Although Morris had been brought up as an Evangelical, he never felt attuned to this creed. He became a Puseyite at Oxford, and, along with many of his contemporaries, was deeply affected by the High Church movement which presaged Anglo-Catholicism. It was assumed by his family at this time that he would go into the Church: Morris and his friends considered forming a monastic brotherhood, but the idea was not pursued, and in fact Dixon and Fulford were the only members of the group finally to take holy orders – Dixon was curate of St Mary's, Lambeth, by the time he officiated at Morris's wedding in Oxford.

Instead, another Brotherhood, that of the Pre-Raphaelites, emerged as a crucial formative influence on Morris at this time. Morris became acquainted with the Pre-Raphaelites through their magazine, *The Germ*, and through John Ruskin's *Modern Painters* and his *Edinburgh Lectures* (1854). Of all the contemporary writers read and discussed by Morris and his friends, Ruskin was undoubtedly the most important, his ideas coming as a total revelation. Ruskin's *The Stones of Venice* (1853) with its view that medieval buildings reflected the freedom of the workman, later to be dispelled by the Renaissance with its ultimately destructive division between architect and craftsman, made a substantial contribution towards Morris's later artistic vision: the medieval workman deriving genuine pleasure from his work remained the prototype for Morris's concept of the modern craftsman/designer. Forty years later he acknowledged his debt to Ruskin in this respect in his own preface to his Kelmscott Press's reprint of 'On the Nature of Gothic' from *The Stones of Venice*: 'it seemed to point out a new road on which the world should travel. The lesson that Ruskin here teaches us is that art is the expression of man's pleasure in his labour.'

Overleaf left: Snake's-head chintz, fritillaries abounded at Iffley, Oxford.

Overleaf right: Evenlode chintz, 1883

Other authors who exerted a strong influence on Morris at Oxford and continued to do so throughout his life were Shakespeare, Chaucer, the chronicler Froissart, and Malory: the latter's *Morte d'Arthur*, with its compelling blend of medieval romance, chivalry and mysticism, made a powerful impact on both Morris and Burne-Jones and remained a perennial source of inspiration to them both – during a vacation visit to Burne-Jones's home, Morris purchased the 1817 edition by Southey of the *Morte d'Arthur* and had it specially bound in white vellum. As well as Ruskin, influential contemporaries included Carlyle (especially in *Past and Present*, with its striking contrast between the peaceful, ordered existence of a 12th century monastery and the ugly hurly-burly of the 19th century), Kingsley, Browning and Tennyson. On the latter's death in 1892 Morris himself would be offered the Poet Laureateship but would turn it down, just as he did the invitation to stand as Oxford Professor of Poetry in 1877 following Matthew Arnold's completion of his tenure.

Morris was already writing poetry as an undergraduate, to enthusiastic response from his friends, and he published a selection of the best of his early verse in *The Defence of Guinevere* in 1858. Following his 21st birthday in 1855 he came into a substantial £900 annuity, which enabled him to enter upon another literary venture, providing the finance for a monthly student review, *The Oxford and Cambridge Magazine*, which ran to 12 issues from January 1856 under the editorship of Fulford, who was paid £100 per annum. This vehicle for Morris's and his friends' ideas and enthusiasms was published in London by Bell and Daldy at 1s a copy and was well thought of by Ruskin and Tennyson, although Morris himself would describe it 30 years later as 'very young indeed'.

Left: *William Morris, aged 23.*

Right: *Millais's* Return of the Dove to the Ark, *1851*

Duke Humphrey's Library in the Bodleian, with its superb collection of medieval illuminated manuscripts, offered Morris every facility to develop an interest which would later find expression in his own fine work as an illuminator and calligrapher, and in the magnificent personal collection of early manuscripts which he built up. Oxford and the surrounding countryside also provided Morris with ample opportunity to continue at first hand his interest in flowers and plants: the fritillary or snake's-head grew profusely in the grass meadows around Oxford, especially at Iffley, and wild tulips could be found by the Cherwell south of the Botanic Gardens — both flowers were favourites of Morris and featured prominently in later designs.

During vacations Morris visited northern France and the Low Countries, where he discovered for himself the beauty of the early Gothic cathedrals at Chartres, Rouen, Beauvais and Amiens (he contributed an essay on these to *The Oxford and Cambridge Magazine*), and the paintings of Van Eyck and Memling. At home, it was the paintings of the Pre-Raphaelites that evoked special interest in both Morris and Burne-Jones. Holman Hunt's *The Awakened Conscience* and *The Light of the World* were shown at the Royal Academy's summer exhibition in 1854, and Millais's *Return of the Dove to the Ark* was exhibited at Wyatt's in Oxford's High Street. The two friends also saw Pre-Raphaelite paintings in Mr Coombe's collection at the Clarendon Press, and work by Millais and Ford Madox Brown

in Mr Windus's collection in London, at Tottenham Green. They saw *The Light of the World* again, along with several other Pre-Raphaelite paintings, in Paris while on holiday in France in 1855. Now on the brink of their respective artistic careers, they would soon come into direct contact with the magnetic founder of the Pre-Raphaelite Brotherhood, Dante Gabriel Rossetti.

Figure of Guinevere, drawing and watercolour by William Morris, c. 1858

Chapter Two

APPRENTICESHIP (1856-8)

After taking his degree, Morris was articled to the architect, G. E. Street, a leading figure in the Gothic Revival, but, frustrated by office routine, was to stay only for a few months. However, while working there he met Philip Webb, with whom he was to enjoy many a successful collaboration, and architecture was to remain a passion. In 1856 he moved to London where he shared lodgings with Burne-Jones; unable to find suitable furniture, they designed their own, a move which was ultimately to lead to the formation of 'The Firm'. The two became friends with Ruskin and Rossetti, and at Rossetti's suggestion Morris joined the group of young artists who were decorating the Oxford Union debating hall.

On completing his studies at Oxford, Morris decided against taking holy orders, to the intense disappointment of his mother, to whom he wrote a letter of explanation in November 1855. In fact the decision had been taken while on holiday with Burne-Jones in France the previous summer. The two young men resolved to dedicate their careers to the arts; Burne-Jones went to London to study painting, and Morris, already deeply interested in architecture, became articled to George Edmund Street in Oxford.

Street, who had been architect to the diocese of Oxford since 1852, was a leading figure of the Gothic Revival, and he is now probably best known for the Law Courts in London's Strand, on which he started work in 1866.

Morris did not take well to the practicalities of architectural training — he felt restricted by office routine, and frustrated by the 'second-hand' nature of the work he was given to do; not surprisingly, as it seems he spent most of his time in Street's office copying a drawing of the doorway of St Augustine's Church, Canterbury. Although he only stayed nine months with Street, the two men got to know each other well (Street was only 10 years Morris's senior); they visited Lille together, to deliver Street's completed competition designs for the cathedral there. Street's vision of the architect as not just a builder but a painter, glass designer and fabric worker as well, in other words as an all-round artist, undoubtedly made an important contribution to the view of the complete, integrated artist/craftsman towards which Morris was moving. Interestingly, Street was very knowledgeable about historic textiles, which would later feature so importantly in Morris's work, and in 1848 had published a book on ecclesiastical embroidery with Agnes Blencowe, co-founder with Street's sister of the Ladies Ecclesiastical Embroidery Society.

Left: Church of SS Philip and James, Oxford, designed by G.E. Street

Although Morris did not complete his architectural training, his time with Street moulded the extraordinary breadth of his vision as a designer, and he remained passionately interested in architecture all his life. He always considered the architect to be the supreme master craftsman, and the decorative arts to have meaning only in relation to architecture. In his Arts and Crafts essay on 'Textiles' (1889) (see page 108) he remarked that 'the Japanese have no architectural, and therefore no decorative, instinct': while admiring the brilliance of Japanese craftsmanship, he saw Japanese works of art as 'mere wonderful toys . . . outside the pale of the evolution of art . . . which . . . cannot be carried on without the architectural sense that connects it with the history of mankind'.

In practical terms, too, much of Morris's work as an interior designer would be done in close collaboration with one particular architect, Philip Webb – a partnership which would be as resoundingly successful and productive as that of the architect Lutyens with the great lady gardener, Gertrude Jekyll. Webb was Street's senior clerk when Morris joined the Oxford office, and their meeting was crucial to them both: they became lifelong friends and collaborated on many projects together. Years later, Webb gave Morris's daughter May an amusing account of her father as he recalled him in his days as an apprentice: 'I was told . . . in the office to help your Father, and this was done pleasantly and easily as we understood each other at once. When a

Above: *Philip Webb, Morris's lifelong friend and collaborator*

difficult point arose your Father would beat his head with his fists, till I thought it would stun him.' (This intense, violent physical reaction, to which Morris often resorted as a way of releasing frustrated energies, was often remarked upon by those who knew him.) Webb also expressed amazement at the constructiveness of Morris's criticism while he was still only a young trainee, anticipating his later quite extraordinary ability to grasp at once principles and techniques which would normally take a long time to learn.

Webb and Morris were kindred spirits in a number of ways. Three years Morris's senior, Webb was born and grew up in Oxford, and shared Morris's devotion to the city and the beauties of its architecture. Like Morris, too, Webb involved himself totally in all he

throughout. The degree of care he took over his houses can be seen in his correspondence with his clients: for example, when he was working on Standen, the house near East Grinstead in West Sussex commissioned by the solicitor Mr J. S. Beale, for which Morris would provide the decorations (see page 112), Webb wrote a letter to his client's daughter Amy discussing in the minutest detail the arrangement of the furniture in her bedroom, illustrating the various options with sketches.

When Street moved his office to London, to Montagu Place, Bloomsbury, Morris went with him, and shared digs with Burne-Jones, first in Upper Gordon Street, Bloomsbury, then at 17 Red Lion Square. These rooms had originally been occupied by Rossetti, whom Burne-Jones had met at the Working Men's College in Great Ormond Street. Rossetti, who taught at the College, as did the revered Ruskin and Ford Madox Brown, another leading light of the Pre-Raphaelite Brotherhood, became a friend and mentor to both Burne-Jones and Morris, impressing them with his belief that society should fall into just two halves: painters, and people to buy their pictures. The two friends joined Rossetti's Hogarth Club, whose distinguished membership included Brown, Holman Hunt, Spencer Stanhope, Arthur Hughes, Street, Benjamin Woodward, G. F. Bodley and Sir Frederic Leighton. Rossetti, obviously aware of Morris's private means, encouraged him to buy friends' pictures: it was on his advice that Morris purchased Brown's *Hayfield* and Arthur

did, personally supervising every detail of a job. His architectural practice, while highly successful, remained very small, as he would only agree to take on one commission at a time, so that he could give it his undivided attention

Hughes's *April Love*, which he had seen in the 1856 Royal Academy summer exhibition, along with Hunt's *The Scapegoat*, Millais's *Autumn Leaves* and Wallis's *Death of Chatterton*.

A turning-point for Morris as designer/craftsman came when he and Burne-Jones found that they were quite unable to find any furniture they liked sufficiently to furnish their rooms in Red Lion Square. So they designed their own, thus establishing a trend which would be followed again for the decoration of Morris's next home, the Red House, and would ultimately result in the formation of the firm of Morris, Marshall, Faulkner and Co.

Morris's designs, which could have come straight out of the Middle Ages — aptly described by Rossetti as 'incubi and succubi' — were made by a local carpenter in plain deal, which provided a perfect base for decoration. There was a large round table, and chairs with backs painted by Rossetti, who chose to depict scenes from Morris's own poems, 'Gwendolen in the Tower' and 'The Arming of a Knight'. Philip Webb designed a wardrobe which Burne-Jones decorated with scenes from Chaucer's *Prioress's Tale*, and later gave to Morris for the Red House as a wedding present; it is now in the Ashmolean Museum, Oxford. May Morris later wrote of this wardrobe: 'I never watch the gold of sunset behind the silhouette of the black tree-branches in my fruit orchard without being reminded of the similar effect in the background of this picture on the larger door. We children, by the by, used to say that the Chaucer at the bottom of it was "Uncle Ned" [Burne-Jones] himself.'

The best-known piece of furniture designed for Red Lion Square was an enormous settle with a long seat and three cupboards above, again painted jointly by Rossetti and Burne-Jones, this time with scenes from the story of Dante's love for Beatrice: this also went to the Red House, and is now in the Victoria and Albert Museum.

These pieces represent the sole extent of Morris's own furniture design; although Morris and Co. was noted for its distinctive furniture, this was never designed by Morris himself, but usually by Philip Webb, later with George Jack.

Left: April Love *by Arthur Hughes, purchased by Morris in 1856*

Below: The settle from Red Lion Square, *in the sitting room at the Red House*

It was at this time, too, that Morris produced a piece of work which is his only known personal contribution to another of the decorative arts, embroidery, for which his company would also be famous. Although Morris made a variety of designs for embroidered work, and his daughter May became an outstanding embroideress and embroidery designer (see page 104), the so-called 'If I Can' embroidery of 1857 is unique to Morris himself. It is interesting not only for this reason, but for all that it reveals about Morris's approach to design generally. He was already putting into practice the belief that would remain with him all his life, and which would be the guiding principle of all his design work, that is, that the designer should be totally familiar in practical terms with the techniques of his chosen medium, and should never design anything that he could not produce with his own hands. Just as over 20 years later, by that time an established designer of great note, Morris taught himself to weave, now, on the threshold of his design career, he taught himself to embroider, on a wooden frame specially made up to an old pattern, using wools which he had dyed by an elderly French dyer who lived in the neighbourhood of Red Lion Square. 'If I Can', the motto adapted from the 'Als Ich Kanne' of Van Eyck, whose work Morris had admired

Left: A detail from the 'If I Can' embroidered wall hanging, designed and worked in wools on linen by William Morris in 1857. It hangs at Kelmscott Manor

in the Low Countries, well expresses the determination and tenacity which Morris brought to all his enterprises; it featured again in another context at the Red House, in the garden porch tiles, and on stained glass and the drawing-room frescoes.

The 'If I Can' embroidery was worked in wool, in brick stitch, to cover the linen canvas completely. The resulting effect, with its dense texture, is similar to tapestry, and Morris undoubtedly made the embroidery as an experiment in recreating the fabric hangings of the Middle Ages which he himself always preferred to paper as a wall covering. The embroidery now hangs in the way Morris intended it to do, on a wall in the Green Room at Kelmscott Manor. Though faded now, the piece is of great interest, not least as an early example of the use of repeat patterning which Morris would put to such good effect in his later textiles and wallpapers: the repeat element can be clearly seen in the charmingly naive pattern of highly stylized birds and standard trees bearing raised fruit, as well as the scrolls displaying the motto.

In connection with these early experiments with embroidery, it is interesting to observe how Morris enlisted the help of the accommodating maid at Red Lion Square, nicknamed 'Red Lion Mary', with embroidery work. After Morris's marriage, his wife, her sister and other friends would be drawn in to help with embroidery and decorative work in the same way, and, indeed, it was Morris's practice throughout his life to make best use of available staff by

Above: The Dwellers at Eyr, *Morris's first decorated calligraphic manuscript, 1869. His interest in illumination dated from his Oxford days*

putting them to work on things for which they often had no previous training or experience. He was clearly as inspired in his teaching of others as he was of himself.

Another significant area which Morris was exploring at this time was that of illumination. He spent a great deal of time poring over the medieval illuminated manuscripts in the British Musuem, just as he had in the Bodleian Library in Oxford; many of his favourite design motifs would later be derived from the exquisite illuminated miniatures and decorative borders which he observed there. He became highly proficient himself in the art of illuminating: Ruskin, whom Morris and Burne-Jones had been thrilled to meet on coming to live in London, and of whom they now saw a good deal – enough for Ruskin to refer to them as 'my dear boys' – wrote a letter to the Keeper of Manuscripts at the British Museum recommending Morris's ability as an illuminator. Rossetti also remarked on Morris's illuminating work as 'quite unrivalled by anything modern that I know'.

In fact Morris's skills as an artist found ideal expression in illuminated decoration, far more so than they ever did in painting on canvas. So it is perhaps ironic that, under Rossetti's direct influence, Morris at this time decided to give up architecture and devote himself to becoming a painter.

His first painting venture was also instigated by Rossetti, who in 1857 had been invited by the Irish architect Benjamin Woodward, perhaps best known for the University Museum at Oxford, to organize the decoration of his current project, the new Oxford Union debating hall. Morris joined the team of young painters, including Hughes, Stanhope, Burne-Jones, Hungerford Pollen, Val Prinsep and Alexander Munro, assembled by Rossetti to help him implement his scheme of decorating the 10 bays between the circular windows in the gallery with scenes from Malory's *Morte d'Arthur*, in tempera.

The job was organized on an amateur basis, in that the artists were not paid a fee, just their expenses for materials and accommodation, and the work was conducted in a light-hearted, convivial atmosphere: Charles Faulkner, now a Fellow of University College, dropped in to lend a hand in the afternoons, and Webb came up from London at weekends to help with the roof decorations. In this spirit of enthusiasm, and in a number of other respects, the enterprise anticipated Morris's later work. First of all, it was undertaken in collaboration with like-minded friends; it was on a similar collaboration that Morris's firm would be founded a few years later. Secondly, the Union murals scheme demonstrated Morris's outstanding ability to concentrate hard and work fast: each artist was allocated a theme from the story of the knights of the Round Table, and Morris finished his — the story of Sir Palomydes's unrequited love for La Belle Iseult — first, going on to help to decorate the roof while the others were still completing their work. Thirdly, and perhaps most significantly, Morris went to a great deal of trouble to ensure that he turned out as good a job as possible.

The artists used each other as models, a practice which would recur as a feature of the stained glass designs produced by Morris's firm, but Morris actually had a suit of armour specially made by a local blacksmith to his own design, so that he could use it to work from on his mural. The suit is now lost, but the helmet, with its visor and chainmail gorget, and the sword, can be seen on permanent display in the William Morris Gallery. Burne-Jones later recalled the hilarious scene when Morris first tried on the helmet and the visor would not lift, though fortunately later, once he had got used to the mechanism, he was delighted with the armour, to the extent of wearing it at dinner.

The finished murals were highly acclaimed, and were compared in the brightness and purity of their colours to the pages of an illuminated manuscript. Unfortunately, however, the amateur enthusiasm with which they were executed also had its negative side: the painting had been done straight on to damp, untreated plaster, and deteriorated very quickly, until the murals were virtually unrecognizable. Somewhat ironically, 20 years later Morris and Co. would be asked to undertake the redecoration of the roof.

Below: *The Oxford Union debating hall, showing the murals Morris worked on*

'Si Je Puis' stained glass on the upper landing, the Red House

Chapter Three

MARRIAGE AND THE RED HOUSE (1859-61)

While he was working on the Oxford Union murals, Rossetti introduced Morris to Jane Burden, the daughter of an Oxford groom and a great beauty. They were married in 1859, and Morris commissioned Philip Webb to design their first home. This was the Red House, near Bexleyheath in Kent; it was a romantic red-brick building of an irregular picturesque shape, with all the rooms overlooking the garden. It was not a particularly large house, but gave the impression of being so, and its uncluttered whitewashed interior was in stark contrast to the average Victorian home. 'Top [Morris] is slowly making Red House the beautifullest place on earth', wrote Edward Burne-Jones in 1862.

41

While working in Oxford on the Union murals, Morris was introduced by Rossetti to Jane Burden, the daughter of an Oxford groom living in Holywell Street. Jane was first seen by the friends with her sister at the theatre, and one can imagine the impact she made on them: tall and slender, with abundant tresses of thick black wavy hair framing a pale face with a reticent and mysterious expression in the melancholy, deep-set eyes below heavy brows, her stately, brooding style of beauty was the very personification of the Pre-Raphaelite ideal. In 1869, when Morris and Jane had been married for 10 years and were living 'over the shop' in Queen Square, the novelist Henry James called to see them, and his account of the visit, in a letter to his sister, conveys the very strong impression Jane Morris made on him:

> Such a wife! Je n'en reviens pas — she haunts me still. A figure cut out of a missal — out of one of Rossetti's or Hunt's pictures — to say this gives but a faint idea of her, because when such an image puts on flesh and blood, it is an apparition of fearful and wonderful intensity. It's hard to say whether she's a grand synthesis of all the Pre-Raphaelite pictures ever made — or they a "keen analysis" of her — whether she's an original or a copy. In either case she's a wonder.

And this was despite the fact that on the occasion James refers to, Jane had a raging toothache and had to lie on the sofa all evening, her face covered with a handkerchief, while Morris gave a reading of his poetry.

In fact it seems likely that Rossetti loved Jane from the first, although at the time of their meeting he was already engaged to his favourite model, Lizzie Siddal. After Lizzie's death in 1862, a long-standing affair developed between Jane and Rossetti, inspiring some of his most outstanding poems, such as 'The Portrait' (1868), and paintings. He drew and painted Jane obsessively, and some particularly fine examples, including the stunning oil portrait, 'The Blue Silk Dress', can be seen in the Panelled Room and adjoining Closet at Kelmscott Manor. The relationship must certainly have caused Morris great anguish, and may well have contributed, too, to his throwing himself into his work with such concentration and dedication, to escape from his personal problems. Certainly his hyper-energy was always in marked contrast with the languid pose most commonly associated with Jane, who enjoyed chronic poor health, in the manner of many of the ladies of the Victorian era (although she outlived Morris by 20 years), and was all too often to be found in the invalid pose described by Henry James.

However, all this was to come. In Oxford during the work on the Union murals Jane posed for Morris as Iseult/ Guinevere, and interestingly, Morris's painting in oils of her in this role is the only extant example of his work in this

Right: The Blue Silk Dress, Rossetti's portrait of Jane Morris aged 26

medium. Despite Morris's resolve in these early days to become a painter, he never felt truly at home painting on canvas; he was much more in his natural element with painting as decoration, on furniture and ceilings, and in illumination work. In fact Philip Webb claimed that Morris found the portrait of Jane a struggle, and Rossetti and Brown finished it off for him.

The wedding

Although Morris's family clearly disapproved of the match, for none of them attended the wedding at St Michael's, Oxford, Jane Burden and William Morris were married on 26 April 1859. It was in this month that Webb finalized the plans for the house that was to be the

Above: Burne-Jones's sketch of Morris with his daughters, c. 1865

Below: Rossetti's coloured chalk drawings of Jenny (left) and May Morris, 1872, now at Kelmscott Manor

Morrises' first home, overlooking the Cray Valley at Upton near Bexleyheath in Kent, three miles from Abbey Wood station, and only 10 miles from London. Morris had asked his friend to undertake the job the previous summer, during a boating trip in Normandy, and the commission had encouraged Webb to set up in practice on his own. His new office was at 7 Great Ormond Street, and the Morrises lived temporarily at no. 41 before moving to the completed Red House in 1860.

True vocation

There now began an immensely happy and productive period in Morris's life. The Red House acted as a kind of catalyst for him in his career, for it was as a result of work on the house itself that he found his true vocation as a designer. The Red House, too, saw the birth of both the daughters who would mean so much to Morris, and whom he would later affectionately and proudly describe as 'very sympathetic with me as to my aims in life'. Jane, always known as Jenny, was born in January 1861, and her sister Mary, always called May, a year later. A delightful informal sketch by Burne-Jones of Morris sitting at a table feeding the two curly-haired infants on his lap charmingly illustrates what an excellent father Morris must have been.

The Red House was the first of Morris's dream houses. All his homes were special to him, and significant in any assessment of his work, because they were places to work as well as live in, and Morris believed that attractive

Above: The Red House, from a drawing by H.P. Clifford

surroundings were essential for the production of good work. The Red House was so named for the red brick of which it was built. The use of brick was innovatory at a time when stucco was still the fashion, and although Webb was influenced to some extent by Pugin, Street and Butterfield, the outstanding architects of his day, his special method of meeting his friend and client's requirements made the house a landmark in English domestic architecture, as well as setting the pattern for lifelong collaboration between Morris the designer and Webb the architect.

The Red House was an intensely romantic house, very medieval in spirit, but at the same time highly functional and practical. It was built in a two-storied L-shape, the line of its high-pitched red-tiled roof deliberately irregular, with some gables vertical, some hipped or half-hipped. The well-

Above: The stairwell, the Red House. The ceiling was decorated by Morris

house in the square well-court had a steep conical tiled roof. A tower in the inner angle of the 'L' contained the great open staircase, and the external angle on the second floor was filled by the magnificent drawing room, which featured a huge patterned brick chimneypiece bearing the motto 'Ars longa vita brevis' (Life is brief but art endures). The garden, with its trellis and grassy walks dividing up the different areas, was equally romantic and evocative of the Middle Ages. In the account of her beloved childhood home which she gives in her memoir of her father and his work, May Morris includes a description of the garden, which must have meant as much to the Morrises as the house itself: 'The garden that graced this pleasant home was

characteristic, so happily English in its sweetness and freshness, with its rose-hedges and lavender and rosemary borderings to the flower-beds, its alley and bowling-green, and the orchard-walks among the apple-trees.' In fact the apple trees in the orchard grew so near the house that the fruit would fall in through windows left open on summer evenings. All the rooms at the Red House overlooked the garden, giving Morris every opportunity to observe from indoors as well as outside, 'the birds, flowers and trees which would prove such a rich source of inspiration to him in his pattern-designing.

The Morrises used to hold open house for friends at weekends, always highly enjoyable for excursions into the lovely surrounding countryside during the day and animated discussions as well as lively fun in the evenings. An important feature of a visit to the Red House was the way guests would be invited to participate in the schemes for its decoration. The interior of the Red House, with its plain distempered walls and open beams, was deliberately uncluttered, in total contrast to the overcrowded rooms characteristic of the typical Victorian home. When it came to furnishing and decorating the house, as previously in Red Lion Square, Morris could find nothing to his taste. So, enlisting the help of his wife and their friends, he set about making the Red House the most beautiful home in England.

Frescoes

Morris and Jane painted the drawing room ceiling, and posed as Sir Degravaunt and his bride for the series of seven frescoes portraying the Sir Degravaunt story from the Arthurian cycle, designed by Morris and Burne-Jones for the walls. Three of these would be completed by Burne-Jones, painted in tempera, with decoration by Morris below of birds and trees and the 'If I Can' motto, to which Rossetti jokingly added his own 'As I Can't'. Scenes from the legend of Troy were planned for the staircase and hall – one, portraying a great ship carrying the Greek heroes would be executed by Burne-Jones – and from the *Nibelungen-lied* for a large cupboard: thus the Arthurian, Ancient Greek and Teutonic sagas, all of which meant so much to Morris, were drawn together under the same roof.

Morris and Burne-Jones also designed stained glass for the Red House, another innovation in domestic building at that time. One window depicted a green-robed, blind-folded figure of Fortune holding a wheel; another showed Love in a red gown standing by a stream against a background of flames.

Both Jane Morris and her sister Bessie (who was never popular with Morris, but was tolerated by him) were proficient in embroidery: May Morris proudly described her mother as 'past-mistress in her art', and Elizabeth Burden was sufficiently talented to become a teacher at the Royal School of Art Needlework in the 1870s. Jane Morris embroidered to her husband's design the wall hangings for the main bedroom at the Red House, where none of the rooms were papered. The design, a simple outline daisy clump pattern, was executed in couched and laid stitching in bright red and yellow wools on coarse, dark blue serge which Jane found in a London shop. Subsequently, similar material would be specially supplied to Morris for embroidery work by a firm of Yorkshire manufacturers. The daisy motif, inspired by an illuminated manuscript of a Froissart chronicle Morris had seen in the British Museum (Harl. MSS 4379/80), was a favourite with him and recurred frequently in his designs for tiles and stained glass, and, most importantly in

Above: Daisy *embroidered hanging. Designed by Morris and executed by Jane Morris and others, 1860*

one of his early wallpaper designs (see pages 68–70). The *Daisy* wall hangings can now be seen in the Screens Passage of the North Hall at Kelmscott Manor, and another embroidery done for the Red House, of sunflowers, hangs in the North Attic.

A more ambitious embroidery scheme for the Red House, again for wall hangings, and this time for the dining room, was a series of 12 figure panels, designed to imitate tapestry, and indeed reminiscent of the later *Orchard* tapestry (see page 101). These were worked on plain linen in wool, silk and gold thread, using the same brick stitch technique as in Morris's 'If I Can' embroidery (see pages 36–37). Panels

for the figure of St Catherine, appliqué on brown velvet, worked by Jane Morris, and the figure of Penelope, on green serge, worked by Bessie, also hang at Kelmscott Manor.

Burne-Jones recalls painting tiles for the Red House fireplaces, and Philip Webb, who as already mentioned would go on to design much of Morris's furniture, now produced furniture designs for the Red House. A fine round table he designed at this time stands in the Tapestry Room at Kelmscott Manor, and he also designed chairs and beds as well as smaller items – grates and fire-irons, metal candlesticks and table glass manufactured by Powells of Whitefriars. Other furniture was brought from Red Lion Square, including the great settle which now had the top railed in to act as a music gallery, with a set of steps ascending to it.

In the course of all the activity on work for the Red House, it occurred to Morris and his friends that others must find themselves in the same situation of being able to find nothing to their taste in terms of house furnishing and decoration. It was from this growing conviction that the idea of the firm of Morris, Marshall, Faulkner and Co. was born. The decoration of the Red House can thus truly be said to have been a microcosm of all the design activities that were to come.

Right: Three of the embroidered figure panels designed for the Red House, c. 1861 and made into a screen for the Earl of Carlisle at Castle Howard in 1889

Chapter Four

THE FIRM (1861-74)

Morris, Marshall, Faulkner & Co. grew out of the combined efforts of the friends who helped Morris with the decorating and furnishing of the Red House. The seven founder members set themselves up as an artists' cooperative with the intention of producing everything necessary to decorate a house. They were amateurs in the best sense of the word, but in true amateur fashion the financial side of the business was chaotic. Their first products were ecclesiastical embroideries and stained glass, both of which were to win them gold medals at the International Exhibition in 1862. Hand-painted tiles, furniture and wallpapers followed, and it was not long before the Firm was able to offer a complete interior decorating service.

Vine and Grapes; *cartoon for stained glass, Jesus College, Cambridge, probably by William Morris, 1872–4*

It was in 1861 that Morris embarked upon his professional career as a designer, with the formation of the firm of Morris, Marshall, Faulkner and Co. Peter Marshall, a surveyor and sanitary engineer, was a friend of Ford Madox Brown, and Charles Faulkner, Morris's friend from Oxford days, had come to London to work as a civil engineer. Burne-Jones, Rossetti, Brown and Webb made up the complement of seven founder members.

The notion of the Firm emerged, as already seen, from the collaborative work done at the Red House; it was not the brainchild of any one partner, but seems to have evolved spontaneously as the result of general discussion among all of them. What is certain is that it was founded on a shoestring; as Morris's biographer J. W. Mackail put it, 'Seldom has a business been begun on a smaller capital.' Each member held a £1 share (later increased to £20), and Morris's mother, now living at Leyton, put up an initial unsecured loan of £100. Faulkner, who looked after the accounts, and Morris each received an annual salary of £150, but otherwise work was paid for on a piece system.

The Firm was set up as a co-operative of artists producing their own designs for limited hand production, an embodiment of Morris's ideal of the designer/craftsman. It was thus based on amateur enthusiasm in the best and most productive sense, with a very strong degree of initial commitment. A letter written by Faulkner to a friend at the time conveys this in exuberant terms.

Below: Morris in his working smock

I don't know whether you have heard of our firm before from me or anyone else. If not, I may just as well tell you that it is composed of Brown, Rossetti, Jones, Webb, Marshall, Morris and Faulkner; that it commenced with a capital which might be considered an infinitesimal of the second order; that it has meetings once or twice a fortnight which have rather the character of a meeting of the "Jolly Masons" or the jolly something elses than of a meeting to discuss business. Beginning at 8 for 9 p.m. they open with the relation of anecdotes which have been culled by members of the firm since the last meeting. This store being exhausted, Topsy [the nickname

given to Morris by friends since Oxford days, on account of his mane of hair] and Brown will perhaps discuss the relative merits of the art of the thirteenth and fifteenth century, and then perhaps after a few more anecdotes business matters will come up about 10 or 11 o'clock and be furiously discussed till 12, 1 or 2.

The Firm's activities were a natural extension of the various decorative schemes executed for the Red House, the intention being to manufacture everything necessary to decorate a home. The inaugural circular of 11 April 1861, which describes the Firm as Fine Art Workmen in Painting, Carving, Furniture and the Metals, gives a clear account of its *raison d'être* and aims, as well as a comprehensive list of its various products and services:

The growth of Decorative Art in this country . . . has now reached a point at which it seems desirable that Artists of reputation should devote their time to it. Although no doubt particular instances of success may be cited, still it must be generally felt that attempts of this kind hitherto have been crude and fragmentary. Up to this time, the want of that supervision, which alone can bring about harmony between the various parts of a successful work, has been increased by the necessarily excessive outlay, consequent on taking one individual artist from his pictorial labours.

The Artists whose names appear above hope by association to do away with this difficulty. Having among their number men of varied qualifications, they will be able to undertake any species of decoration, mural or otherwise, from pictures, properly so-called, down to the consideration of the smallest work susceptible of art beauty. It is anticipated that by such cooperation, the largest amount of what is essentially the artist's work, along with his constant supervision, will be secured at the smallest possible expense, while the work done must necessarily be of a much more complete order, than if any single artist were incidentally employed in the usual manner.

The Artists having for many years been deeply attached to the study of the Decorative Arts of all times and countries, have felt more than most people the want of some one place where they could either obtain or get produced works of a genuine and beautiful character. They have therefore now established themselves as a firm, for the production, by themselves and under their supervision of —

I. Mural Decoration, either in Pictures or in Pattern Work, or merely in the arrangement of Colours, as applied to dwelling-houses, churches, or public buildings.

II. Carving generally, as applied to Architecture.

III. Stained Glass, especially with reference to its harmony with Mural Decoration.

IV. Metal Work in all its branches, including Jewellery.

V. Furniture, either depending for its beauty on its own design, on the application of material hitherto overlooked, or on its conjunction with Figure and Pattern Painting. Under this head is included Embroidery of all kinds, Stamped Leather, and ornamental work in other such materials, besides every article necessary for domestic use. It is only necessary to state further, that work of all the above classes will be estimated for, and executed in a business-like manner; and it is believed that good decoration, involving rather the luxury of taste rather than the luxury of costliness, will be found to be much less expensive than is generally supposed.

The Firm was initially housed in premises at 8 Red Lion Square, just a few doors from where Morris and Burne-Jones had shared digs. The ground floor at no. 8 was occupied by a jeweller, who used to execute jewellery designs for Morris, and the Firm rented the first floor as an office and showroom, with the workshops on the third floor and in the basement, where a small kiln for firing stained glass and tiles was installed. Morris, Marshall, Faulkner and Co. remained in Red Lion Square until 1865 when they moved to more spacious premises nearby at 26 Queen Square, where the office and showroom were on the ground floor, and the ballroom at the end of the yard at the back used as a workshop, with additional workshops in Ormond Yard.

The Morris family moved to live 'above the shop' at Queen Square when Morris reluctantly had to leave the Red House after five happy years there. The move became necessary for a number of reasons: Morris found the commuting exhausting — he had been quite seriously ill in 1864 — and the Red House, which faced north, was very cold in winter (a fact which had not been taken into account when Webb drew up the designs in the exceptionally hot summer of 1859); further, in the early days of the Firm, Morris experienced money worries while he was still getting established, and the Red House became something of a financial burden.

Below: Lamb and Flag *altar frontal, made by the Firm for Llandaff Cathedral*

At Red Lion Square George Campfield, formerly a glass painter with the glass company of Heaton, Butler and Bayne, was employed as the Firm's foreman. Morris had met Campfield at the Working Men's College in Great Ormond Street, and would retain his invaluable services for many years to come. Morris had a remarkable ability to inspire loyalty and devotion in his staff, a fact which must surely have contributed to his success, and George Campfield was still with him in the 1880s when the Morris works moved to Merton Abbey (see page 86).

Above: Rossetti's study of Jane Morris as the Virgin for the Llandaff altarpiece

Ecclesiastical embroideries

As the Firm's activities expanded, extra labour was recruited from Camden Town and from the Boys Home in Euston Road, but to begin with there was considerable involvement of friends and family: there was always a sense of family within Morris's workforce, and employees would quite often introduce friends and relatives who would be taken on to the staff.

From the earliest days of the Firm there was considerable demand for ecclesiastical embroideries; in April 1861 Morris had asked his former tutor at Walthamstow, the Rev. Guy, for a list of clergymen's addresses to whom he might send his first circular. The team of embroideresses handling the work included Jane Morris, her sister Bessie, who worked the outstanding *Lamb and Flag* altar frontal for Llandaff Cathedral, Burne-Jones's wife Georgiana, and Mrs George Campfield. Charles Faulkner's sisters Kate and Lucy, who lived conveniently nearby with their mother in Queen Square, now began their long association with Morris, helping mainly at this time to paint tiles, as did Mrs Burne-Jones.

The negative aspect of this amateur approach was that the business side of the Firm's activities was always in a shambles. When Warington Taylor, who had been introduced by his school-friend Swinburne, was employed by Morris as business manager in 1865, he was appalled to discover just how casually the Firm conducted their affairs. There seemed to be total failure to cost jobs or organize the flow of work, to charge enough or keep proper accounts, or to make the best and most economic use of available labour.

Taylor, who was obviously far better at managing other people's affairs than his own (he himself had fallen on very hard times after being disinherited for converting to Roman Catholicism), did a great deal for Morris, relieving him of much of the burden of the business and enabling him to devote more time to his work. However, until his untimely death from consumption in 1870, Taylor's prolific correspondence with the Firm, most of it directed from Hastings on the South Coast, where he was forced to live for health reasons, constantly urges Morris and his partners to meet schedules and generally work in a more businesslike way.

The Firm received recognition for the outstanding quality of its work very soon after its foundation. 1862 was the year of the International Exhibition at the South Kensington Museum, with which Morris would maintain strong life-long connections, and which now houses an important collection of his work. The Firm entered two classes in the Medieval Court – stained glass, and decorative furniture and tapestries (actually embroideries) – and they won gold medals in both, selling £150 worth of goods at the Exhibition on the strength of this. Both these medal-winning categories were important in the Firm's early output.

Stained glass

Three of the Firm's partners, Rossetti, Brown and Burne-Jones, had been designing stained glass for the well-known firm of James Powell & Sons of Whitefriars from 1856 – an early example of Burne-Jones's work in this medium was the St Frideswide window in Christ Church, Oxford. This experience proved invaluable, for at this time stained glass, like ecclesiastical embroideries, was in great demand as a result of the ritualist revival and expansion of church building, and formed an extremely important part of the Firm's early turnover: for example, of the £3000 total turnover for 1867, £2,300 was for stained glass. After 1870 Rossetti and Brown's contribution dropped very considerably, and Burne-Jones continued as the Firm's principal designer, but from the beginning, Morris himself showed a remarkable instinc-

Left: Tracery light for St Michael's, Tilehurst, by William Morris, 1869

tive grasp of the art of stained glass, although unlike his colleagues he had no previous experience in the medium. Besides designing well over 100 windows (of Marillier's index of the Firm's cartoons for stained glass, now in the Birmingham City Museum and Art Gallery, 129 are attributed to Morris), he provided the backgrounds for many more, often with figures by Burne-Jones, whom, in his memoir of Philip Webb, W. R. Lethaby describes as 'the most fertile and accomplished figure designer, I believe, that we have ever produced', and with birds and animals by Webb himself. Webb had a tremendous talent for drawing wildlife – his assistant George Jack recalled him saying that 'To draw animals you must sympathize with them; you must know what it feels like to be an animal' – and the bear, squirrel, rabbit, dove and owl Webb contributed to the 1862 window depicting Adam and Eve in Paradise for St Martin's, Scarborough (see page 60) are among the most charming examples of his work in this field.

Most importantly, Morris was responsible for the whole process of implementing the stained glass designer's cartoon, or monochrome drawing, and translating it into the actual terms of the medium. A vital part of this was choosing and varying the colours: Morris's unerring colour sense, borne out in all his work, is one of the distinguishing features of the Firm's

stained glass, producing rich, deep tones like those of cloisonné enamel: again in the words of Lethaby, 'Morris's colour-work glows from within; something happens to the several items in association, as when bells chime.' Morris was responsible for selecting the glass itself (the Firm did not have the scope to manufacture its own, a fact which Morris often regretted), for setting the leading lines, overseeing the

Right: *Early 1860s design for a stained glass window by Philip Webb*

painting and directing any retouching, supervising the firing in the basement kiln and finally making up and reviewing the finished window.

Later in life Morris wrote a masterly entry on stained glass for *Chambers' Encyclopaedia*, which itself indirectly provides an excellent account of why Morris glass was so successful and stands out so forcibly beside most other Victorian glass. Morris was concerned with the overall principle of painting *with* rather than *on* glass, stressing the importance of translucent colour unmuddied by excessive shading, simplicity and strength of drawing and composition, and plenty of crisp detail. He described building up the design itself in terms of a mosaic system, areas of pure colour identifying themselves with the meaningful parts of the drawing, with the black leading lines that are intrinsic to stained glass utilized to best effect. Above all, Morris emphasized the importance of respecting the elements of the medium and treating it in terms of its own potential — principles which hold good for his relationship to all the decorative arts with which he was associated. His stained glass was never static but tells an exciting story, rather in the manner of the medieval chronicles he found so compelling.

Certainly, an indication of just how successful Morris stained glass was right from the beginning, is given by the fact that Rossetti's exhibit of seven panels depicting the Parable of the Vineyard at the 1862 International Exhibition was so brilliantly executed that a number of trade competitors, hostile to this firm of amateurs and all that they were setting out to do, tried to get it disqualified on the grounds that it was original medieval glass touched up and remounted. However, they were unsuccessful, and the judges, one of whom was the Clayton of the leading glass firm of Clayton and Bell, were very favourably impressed.

Two years later the Firm was honoured when the South Kensington Museum purchased four stained glass panels for their own collection: a roundel head of *Penelope* and three tall lights, *Chaucer Asleep*, *Dido and Cleopatra* and *Alcestis and Eros*. These were of course vernacular subjects, and stained glass of a domestic nature would often feature in the houses and institutions Morris undertook to decorate, just as it had already at the Red House (see page 47). In 1862 a major series of thirteen panels, portraying the story of Tristram, was commissioned for Harden Grange, Bingley, Yorkshire (these are now at the Cartwright Memorial Hall, Bradford). Burne-Jones also chose an Arthurian theme for his four *Morte d'Arthur* panels for the watercolourist Myles Birket Foster's home, The Hill, at Witley, Surrey, and the Firm provided six windows — five of two lights each, and a bay of six lights — for the Combination Room at Peterhouse, Cambridge, described by May Morris as both 'interesting and intimate'.

Right: Arthur and Lancelot, *cartoon by Morris and Madox Brown, 1862, for a window at Harden Grange, Yorkshire*

Left: *One of Morris's windows for All Saints, Selsley, Gloucestershire, 1862, commissioned by the architect, G.F. Bodley*

An important commission

However, the great majority of Morris stained glass was ecclesiastical. The Firm had got off to a flying start in this respect when the architect G. F. Bodley, enormously impressed by what he had seen on exhibition at South Kensington, commissioned them to provide windows for three of his churches: St Michael's, Brighton; St Martin's on the Hill, Scarborough; All Saints, Selsley, Gloucestershire. All three are outstanding examples of the success with which members of the Firm collaborated on projects. At Brighton, the chancel roof was painted by Morris, Webb and Faulkner, and the windows were designed by Brown and Burne-Jones. Considered by Bodley himself as the finest of all the Firm's

Left: One of Morris's windows for All Saints, Selsley, Gloucestershire, 1862, commissioned by the architect, G.F. Bodley

early stained glass work, these included a rose window of the Creation; four lights depicting the life of Christ; a portrayal of the Nativity with seven roundels surrounding the central Virgin and Child by Burne-Jones; a magnificent rendering of the Archangels by Brown; the three Marys at the tomb in the old vestry; the flight into Egypt and a striking figure of David with his harp in the porch.

At St Martin's on the Hill, Scarborough, Rossetti's award-winning panels of the Parable of the Vineyard, in which Morris and Swinburne make an appearance, were sited below his great east window of the Crucifixion. Rossetti also painted the pulpit with the scene of the Annunciation; the barrel roof above the sanctuary was decorated with a design of rosettes and leaves, and the wall with a brown and yellow net of sunflowers and pomegranates. Of the two windows in the North chapel, one, of St John the Baptist, was by Morris, the other, of Boaz and Ruth in the cornfield, was by Burne-Jones. Burne-Jones also designed the Annunciation for the west rose window, below which was Brown's window of Adam and Eve in Paradise, already mentioned as featuring birds and animals by Webb, and depicting Brown and his wife as Adam and Eve. Brown also contributed a two-light window of St Martin at the west end of the aisle.

All Saints, Selsley

The quality of the glass at All Saints, Selsley, in Gloucestershire, overlooking the Severn Valley, was very likely inspired by the outstanding beauty of the natural surroundings. In the apse, Morris and Burne-Jones respectively contributed windows showing the Ascension and the Resurrection; two windows by Brown depicted the Crucifixion and the Nativity; the beautiful Visitation window was by Rossetti. In another window, showing St Paul preaching at Athens, Morris used his wife as model for one of the listeners in the foreground. This ploy was followed by Rossetti in his Sermon on the Mount window in the South aisle, where he depicted his sister Christina as the Virgin Mary. As with the Oxford Union murals, Morris and his friends liked to use each other and their families as models, giving the resulting work an extra dimension of interest.

In the cartoon for the Sermon on the Mount window, on permanent display in the William Morris Gallery, the different figures are clearly labelled: besides Christina, Rossetti used his favourite model Fanny Cornworth for Mary Magdalene; Swinburne and the painter Simeon Solomon for SS John and James, and the novelist George Meredith as Christ; rumour had it that the art dealer Gambart, whom Rossetti disliked intensely, featured as Judas.

The Sermon on the Mount window illustrates another interesting aspect of the Firm's stained glass work. Despite Warington Taylor's constant cavil that the partners were not making the most of their success in the medium, they did manage to build up a stock of designs which could be repeated. Thus the Sermon on the Mount window was also used at Christ Church, Sunderland, and at Christchurch, Albany Street, Regent's Park, in memory of Rossetti's aunt.

Below: St Paul preaching at Athens, *cartoon for All Saints, Selsley, by William Morris, c 1862*

During his career, William Morris provided stained glass for more than 400 buildings, on a nationwide basis. Later in life, as a direct result of his involvement with the Society for the Protection of Ancient Buildings, he refused further commissions for windows in old churches, on grounds of possible damage done to the original tracery and framework, and because of what he regarded as an unseemly juxtaposition of the new with the original glass. However, he was prepared to make exceptions – for the chancel of St Margaret's, Rottingdean for example, – and certainly stained glass, under the management of George Campfield, continued to be an important part of the output after the move to Merton Abbey.

Tiles

Hand-painted tiles were an important and popular branch of the Firm's activities, both as specially commissioned panels, especially for fireplaces, and as single stock items. They were fired in the basement kiln at Red Lion Square used for stained glass; in fact it was while firing a stained glass piece for Morris that the artist William Frend de Morgan (1839–1917), who had become a close friend and collaborator after being introduced to Morris in the early 1860s, observed that the metallic deposit obtained created an effect very similar to the lustre glazes of Islamic

Right: The Sleeping Beauty, *a set of nine tiles designed by Edward Burne-Jones for Morris, Marshall, Faulkner & Co.*

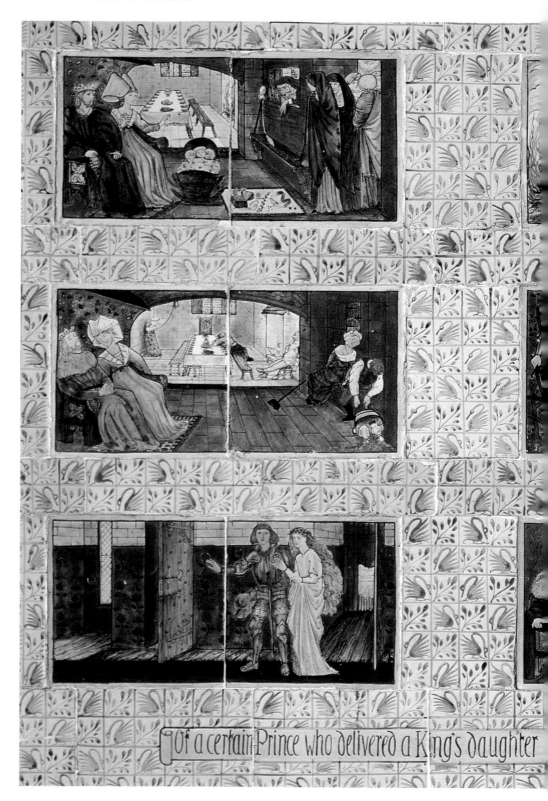

Of a certain Prince who delivered a King's daughter

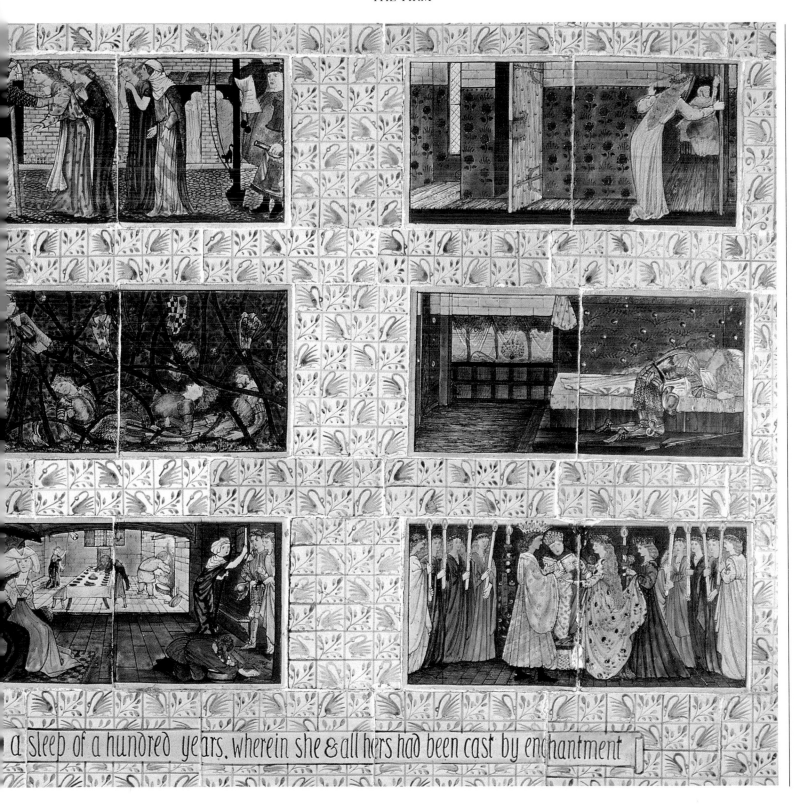

a sleep of a hundred years, wherein she & all hers had been cast by enchantment

Above: Tile painted by William Morris showing Rossetti as Chaucer, reading

pottery which he sought subsequently to achieve, first exclusively on tiles, then on other ornamental wares. With his affinity for bird, animal and interlacing plant form motifs, de Morgan provided the perfect ceramic counterpart to Morris's designs.

Plain tiles were especially imported from Holland for hand-painting, and the Faulkner sisters, Kate and Lucy, did a lot of work on them. In the early days of the Firm, Morris, Burne-Jones and Webb made a number of designs for tiles: Burne-Jones's 'Beauty and the Beast' panel – 'How a Prince who by enchantment was under the form of a

beast became a man again by the love of a certain maiden' – designed for an over-mantel at Birket Foster's Surrey home, was painted by Lucy Faulkner, whose initials appear in the corner of each scene. Burne-Jones also designed tile panels on the 'Cinderella' and 'Sleeping Beauty' themes. Webb's 'Swan' tile, a 16-square pattern of alternating swans and foliage, was popular for panel borders; it was used in this way for the 'Beauty and the Beast', and can be seen in the Green Room fireplace at Kelmscott Manor. A fine example of the Firm's tile panel work, this time designed by Brown in 1873, was the fireplace in the Hall at Queens' College, Cambridge, showing the College's foundresses, Margaret of Anjou and Elizabeth Woodville, as well as its tutelary saints, Bernard and Margaret, and the 12 months of the year.

One of Morris's favourite motifs which he used in a number of linked tile designs was the daisy pattern, which had featured on the embroidered wall hangings described on pages 47–8. Three variations on the daisy theme for tiles can be seen in the William Morris Gallery: one featuring a single clump; another a number of clumps; and a third with a 16-square design in which clumps alternate with single flower-heads.

Furniture

After stained glass, this was the most important part of the Firm's output at the beginning, with a lot of the designs being provided by Philip Webb. Among the award-winning pieces exhibited at South Kensington in 1862 was the so-called *George and Dragon* wall cabinet of mahogany and pinewood on an oak stand, designed by Webb and decorated by Morris with panels vividly recounting the Legend of St George, depicting Jane Morris as the Princess, and providing evidence of Morris's genius as a story-teller. Part of the painting is in transparent colour over gold and silver, and the interior is painted deep 'dragon's blood' red. This cabinet is now in the Victoria and Albert Museum. Other pieces shown by Morris at the International Exhibition included a gilded bookcase depicting the seven stages in family life, and a huge cabinet with shelves, drawers and desk, designed for the architect John Seddon's Whitehall office and decorated by Morris, Burne-Jones, Brown and Rossetti with the theme of King René of Anjou's honeymoon, featuring the arts loved by the King. There was a selection of simpler furniture at the Exhibition, too – an iron bedstead, a sideboard, chest, bookcase, towel-rail and wash-stand.

After his early efforts at 17 Red Lion Square, Morris himself did not design furniture, but retained very strong preferences for simple, traditional designs, in stark contrast with the highly ornate, elaborate and heavy furniture typical of the Victorian era. In this, as in so many other ways, he was in perfect tune with Webb, the Firm's principal furniture designer, who was fond of plain oak furniture stained green or

Below: George and Dragon *cabinet, designed by Philip Webb and painted by William Morris, 1861*

black, sometimes decorated with lacquered leather. Ford Madox Brown also contributed furniture designs, which in the early days of the Firm were made up by Curwen, a Bloomsbury cabinetmaker; some interesting examples of simple green-painted pieces by Brown can be seen in the attics at Kelmscott Manor.

Chairs

One of Webb's most popular designs was the so-called 'Morris' chair, which he adapted from a traditional prototype discovered by Warington Taylor at Herstmonceaux, Sussex, about 1866, in the premises of an old carpenter, Ephraim Colman. It appealed strongly to Taylor, who wrote to Webb describing it and enclosing a sketch. This chair, with its simple frame with arm rests, seat and back cushions, the backs of the arms pierced by holes with brass rods slotted through, enabling adjustment from an upright to reclining position, was tremendously popular. It was up-

holstered in a variety of Morris fabrics – cotton, wool and velvet – and widely copied, for example by Liberty's in London, and in the United States by Graham Stickley at his Craftsman's Workshops in Grand Rapids.

The county of Sussex also provided another important traditional prototype for chairs designed by Morris's Firm – the rush-seated chair, which was produced in plain or ebonized wood to a variety of designs: corner, arm, roundseat and settle, for example. These Sussex chairs were surprisingly inexpensive, sometimes selling for as little as a few shillings, and were enormously popular.

Below: 'Morris' chair, upholstered in Bird *woven wool fabric (see page 10)*

Wallpapers

Although wallpapers were not included in the inaugural prospectus for the Firm, Morris's wallpaper designs are now among the best-known examples of his work, somewhat ironically, as Morris himself preferred embroideries, chintzes or woven wall hangings to the flatness of paper, which, as May Morris recalls, he considered 'makeshift'. As already mentioned, there were no wallpapers at the Red House, and at Kelmscott Manor the rooms were either panelled or hung with tapestries or chintzes. However, Morris did appreciate the valuable contribution wallpapers could make to the Firm's plans to build up a stock of repeatable, as opposed to 'one-off', very expensive items, even though his papers, being hand-printed, were produced in small quantities by today's standards, and often to special commission.

Morris personally designed some 41 wallpapers and five ceiling papers over the length of his career. All the papers were hand-printed in distemper colours from pearwood blocks: pearwood, with its fine grain, was absorbent and easy to carve, but at the same time durable. Morris made some early attempts to print papers himself, in oil colours from

Right: 'Rossetti' chair, Fruit or Pomegranate wallpaper behind. Below: Page from Morris & Co. catalogue, c. 1911

etched zinc plates, then from wooden blocks cut by Barrett of Bethnal Green, but these were unsuccessful in the face of the technical difficulties they presented. Morris then turned to Messrs. Jeffrey of Essex Road, Islington, in whose work he proved to have total confidence: under the personal supervision of Metford Warner, the managing director, Jeffrey and Co. would print all Morris's papers, setting up a special department to handle the work. However, Morris himself, as always, remained closely involved in the production of his designs; the cutter's tracings were always submitted to him

for inspection before printing took place, and he chose the colours personally, and apparently would change them quite arbitrarily at short notice.

Jeffrey and Co.'s ledgers recorded all the wallpaper designs, with details of colour changes, recutting of blocks, etc., and facilitate their dating, together, of course, with the evidence supplied by the Patent Office index of designs registered for copyright purposes, although these refer to finished production, not to the original design.

The hand-printing process, which was an integral part of what Morris was setting out to achieve, was lengthy and laborious, each colour used requiring a separate block (some of the more elaborate designs could involve over 30 of these), and consequently more expensive. The initial trio of wallpapers Morris produced in 1864 cannot have been cheap, as each needed 12 blocks; perhaps this explains why Morris did not return to original wallpaper designs with fine naturalistic patterns until the early 1870s, by which time the Firm's finances were on a more even keel.

These first three wallpapers, the *Trellis*, the *Daisy*, and the *Fruit* or *Pomegranate*, are of great interest in terms of Morris's wallpaper designs generally, as well as being lovely in themselves. The immediate impression

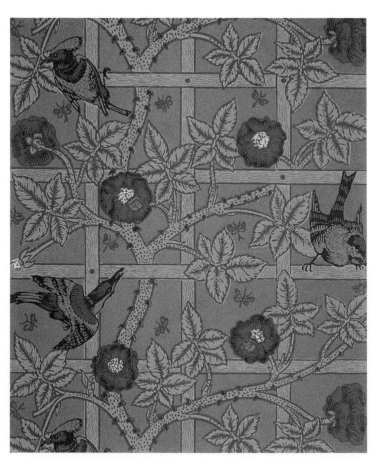

Left: Trellis *(1864), the first wallpaper designed by William Morris*

Right: Fruit *or* Pomegranate, *another very early wallpaper, also 1864*

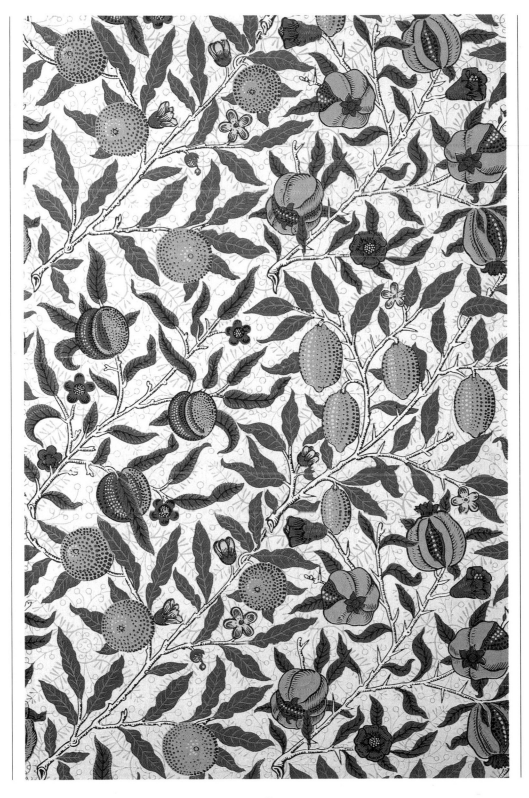

they convey is the sureness of their designer's hand; although they are simple, naive even, in comparison with some of the much more elaborate later patterns, there is nothing tentative about them, and as May Morris said of her father, it was 'as though he had been at the trick for years'. The motifs common to all three papers, of flowers and leaves, with birds in the case of the *Trellis*, and fruit in the case of *Pomegranate*, would provide the basic subject matter of almost all Morris wallpapers, and from the beginning it is significant that his genius lay in creating so many different designs from a limited repertoire of relatively few elements. Most importantly, these early papers illustrate Morris's ability to visualize how a repeat pattern would work in the whole – a tremendous gift, for as May Morris

put it, speaking as a remarkable designer in her own right, 'in designing for a pattern meant to be repeated, you never can tell the effect absolutely till it is seen in mass'. In their different colourways, these papers also show how Morris could make a pattern look completely different, depending on the colour selected, which was always of his own choosing.

William Morris's constant reference to nature for inspiration was one of the ways he ensured his patterns were never derivative or imitative, and this is certainly true as early as the *Trellis*

Below: Daisy, *the first wallpaper produced by the Firm. Typically of Morris's designs, the pattern takes on a new look when reproduced in different colourways*

paper, which was designed though not produced first – it had to wait for Webb to complete the designs for the birds. The idea for the trellis scheme, which provides a uniform rectangular grid contrasting with the continuous motif of the trailing, meandering rose stem, was probably inspired by the rose trellises at the Red House; Bewick's *Birds* was always a major source of design inspiration for Webb, whose birds perched among the roses on the trellis are such a charming feature of this delightful wallpaper. In fact *Trellis* obviously remained a firm personal favourite with Webb, because 30 years later he used it extensively at Standen, where it can still be seen today in the lobby leading to the conservatory, and in the Morning Room corridor. May Morris also remembers it from her bedroom in Queen Square, when she was a child; she used to lie awake disturbed by one of the birds 'because he was thought to be wicked and very alive'.

The daisy motif

The *Daisy*, the first Morris wallpaper to be produced, made use of one of Morris's own favourite motifs, which we saw used in embroidery and on tiles, and which also featured on stained glass quarries (small panels). The *Daisy* remained one of the most popular of Morris wallpapers for half a century. No attempts were made to link or mask the repeats in the pattern, while the background stippling which gives the 'powdered' effect can be seen as an attempt by Morris to give the paper some depth.

The *Fruit* or *Pomegranate* is the most

Above: Design for Jasmine *wallpaper, which was first produced in 1872*

sophisticated of this early group. The pattern is organized around a quartered system, by which the repeat is divided into four equal parts; in each quarter a diagonal stem throws off different fruits and leaves: 'you can almost see the bloom on the lemons and pomegranates and peaches', in the words of May Morris.

It was not until 1871 that Morris returned to original wallpaper designing. Four designs in the Jeffrey records (the *Venetian, Indian, Diaper, Queen Anne*, all about 1868–70), for monochrome wallpapers, were adapted from historical designs, apparently submitted by architects closely connected with the Firm, and do not belong to the category of original design. The first of

the new designs, *Scroll* (1871), is highly reminiscent of the book illumination with which Morris was preoccupied at this time. In his subsequent designs for the period until 1876, flowers and leaves are mostly still rendered in sufficiently naturalistic detail to be readily identifiable, as can be seen in *Jasmine* (1872), *Vine* (1873) and *Marigold* (1875). But compared with the papers of 1864, his designs now immediately strike one as more intricate, full of fluidity and movement, while still retaining a characteristic sense of spontaneous growth and natural freshness: in both the *Larkspur* (1872) and *Willow* (1874), the meandering, loose flowing, informal lines of the design subtly conceal the structure of the repeats. A favourite background to the *Larkspur* was white, which threw up the pattern, with its leafy boughs, blue larkspur sprays, small pink blossoms and buff roses. The *Willow* was and is tremendously popular (it was later adapted as a design for woven silks) and was much used by Morris himself – it can be seen in a modern printing in his bedroom at Kelmscott Manor – although May Morris, while describing it as 'restful and pleasant', did not find it as interesting in its detail as the later *Willow-bough*, which can be seen in Mrs Morris's bedroom at Kelmscott Manor.

Left: Acanthus *wallpaper, 1875: the most ambitious of Morris's designs to date*

Right: Willow, *1874, one of Morris's most popular wallpapers, still widely used*

In another very popular design, the *Acanthus* (1875), which needed 30 blocks to achieve the subtle colour gradation, Morris used a pattern of undulating, complex, scroll-like leaves to create an illusion of depth and counteract the flatness of paper which he did not care for. This problem did not of course arise with fabric, with its natural folds, which is why Morris used relatively few designs interchangeably for both wallpapers and fabrics: notable exceptions included the *Bird and Anemone* of 1882, and Morris's last design, the *Compton*, made for Compton Hall, Mr Lawrence Hodson's home near Wolverhampton.

The total Morris look

As the range of individual decorative facilities offered by the Firm expanded, it was not long before Morris was offering a complete interior decorating service, and it was on this that much of his growing reputation came to be founded.

In 1866 the Firm received two important and highly prestigious commissions which did much for their reputation and for spreading their name, one at the South Kensington Museum and the other at St James's Palace. At South Kensington the brief, masterminded by Webb, was to refurbish the Green Dining-Room (now the William Morris Room). The outstanding feature of this room are the painted figure panels set into the green-stained

Above: The Green Dining-Room at the South Kensington Museum, decorated by the Firm to an 1866 commission

oak panelling, representing the months of the year, alternating with exotic fruit designs on a gold background. These were designed by Burne-Jones and executed by Charles Fairfax-Murray. Above the panelling the walls were covered in cast plaster with a repeat-pattern relief design of olive branches. Webb designed the ceiling with its sharp-leaved decoration, and a frieze in green, red and gold, of dogs pursuing hares, inspired, according to Lethaby, by the font in Newcastle Cathedral. The stained glass windows contained floweret circles by Webb, with figures by Burne-Jones. The whole effect was subtle, restful and restrained.

At St James's Palace the Firm was required to refurbish the Armoury and Tapestry Rooms, and to repaper the Entree Room, the Ballroom and the Banqueting Room. Webb was again responsible for working out the decorative schemes, and a measure of their success was that later, in 1879, Morris would be asked to supply carpets and rugs for these rooms, and to redecorate the Visitors' Entrance and the Grand, Queen's and Ambassadors' Staircases. In 1881 he was invited to redecorate the main suite of state rooms, including the Guard Room, Throne Room, Yellow Room, Blue Room and Boudoir, as well as the Reception and Throne Rooms. The commission would include a specially designed silk damask for the state rooms, hand-painted ceilings and cornices, and a specially designed wallpaper for the staircase.

As Charles Mitchell put it in his article on Morris's work at St James's Palace (*Architectural Review*, January, 1947), 'One of Morris's first achievements was . . . to revolutionize what the inside of a house should look and feel like.' It was during this period that as well as the official commissions, Morris embarked on the collaboration which would result in his decorating a series of houses designed by Philip Webb. Their first major joint commission was a London house for George Howard, later Earl of Carlisle: Morris also decorated the Howards' country homes, Castle Howard in Yorkshire, and Naworth Castle in Cumberland, where the Morrises were frequent guests – a watercolour of Naworth by May Morris hangs in her mother's bedroom at Kelmscott Manor.

The Howards' town house was at 1 Palace Green, described in an article in the *Studio* (October 1898) as 'delightfully situated in a wooded lane opening directly out of the busiest part of High Street, Kensington'. The house was built between 1868 and 1872; Morris was asked to decorate it throughout, which would take him the best part of 10 years to complete. The degree of care and attention he gave to the job is clear from the letters quoted in the second volume of Mackail's biography, from Morris to Mrs George Howard, giving her full accounts of his and Burne Jones's visits to the premises, and consulting closely with her on their

Below: William Morris's bed at Kelmscott Manor, with its embroidered hangings

plans for the decoration. Mrs Howard's boudoir, decorated in red to set off the pearl-greys in Burne-Jones's painting of the Annunciation which hung there, must have been delightful, but the *pièce de résistance* of the house was undoubtedly the panelled dining-room where the highlight was Burne-Jones's frieze of the story of Cupid and Psyche, as told by Morris in *The Earthly Paradise*, his immensely popular collection of stories from medieval, classical, Oriental and Norse legends, the first volume of which was published in 1868. A lavishly illustrated edition with woodcuts by Burne-Jones was planned but never materialized, but it is from the designs made by Burne-Jones for this project that the Howards' frieze was derived. Its 13 panels, executed by Burne-Jones and Walter Crane, and described by the *Studio* magazine as appearing to glow 'like a page of an illuminated missal', are now in the Birmingham City Museum and Art Gallery.

Above: *The Panelled Room at Kelmscott Manor, Morris's country home from 1871*

In total contrast with the grandeur of 1 Palace Green, illustrating equally well in its own way the successful collaboration of Webb and Morris, was the house built and decorated for the artist G. B. Boyce in Glebe Place, Chelsea. Webb created a highly intimate, secluded atmosphere in this small house with its big studio, which Morris reflected in his mellow and harmonious decorative schemes throughout all the rooms.

In 1871 Morris acquired the best-loved of his own homes, Kelmscott Manor, near Lechlade in Gloucestershire. The Morrises' London home at this time was still at Queen Square — they would move the following year to Horrington House at Turnham Green, conveniently situated only 30 minutes' walk from Burne-Jones's home, The

Grange, at Fulham. Right from the beginning the cramped conditions at Queen Square must have coloured Morris's feelings for his country retreat, set in the sleepy little village among peaceful water meadows of the Thames, and although he never actually owned Kelmscott Manor – he took out a joint tenancy with Rossetti in 1871 – the house had a tremendous influence on his work as a designer, in both general and specific ways. He gives a delightful, sensitive description of Kelmscott Manor and all it meant to him in his Utopian romance *News from Nowhere* – C. M. Gere made an evocative drawing of the east front of the Manor for the frontispiece (see page 114) – and in his correspondence he frequently refers in loving detail to the flowers and birds which helped to make the place such a joy. His daughter May paid a charming tribute to Kelmscott Manor when she described one of her father's chintz designs, the *Wild Tulip*, as 'all Kelmscott to me'.

The first three years of the tenancy of

Above: *Kelmscott Manor, showing the east front of the house*

Left: *The Morris and Burne-Jones children at The Grange, Fulham, 1874*

Kelmscott Manor were overshadowed for Morris by the presence of Rossetti, still involved in his affair with Jane. However, Morris was able to escape to Iceland during this time; he had been studying Icelandic, and the Norse sagas with E. Magnusson, whom he had met in 1870, and his first visit to Iceland in 1871 made a powerful impact on him.

In 1874 Rossetti left Kelmscott Manor, which remained Morris's country home until the end of his life. His widow purchased it in 1913 and in 1939 it was left by May Morris to Oxford University. In 1962, however, the trust was proved invalid and the house passed to the Society of Antiquaries, who have made it a shrine to Morris which can be visited by the public on certain days.

Chapter Five

MORRIS AND CO. (1875-96)

In 1875 the Firm was reorganized under Morris's sole direction and its name was changed to Morris and Co. New large showrooms were acquired on the corner of Oxford Street and North Audley Street and the former dye-house, the old larder at the Queen Square premises, was exchanged for spacious workshops at Merton Abbey, only seven miles from Charing Cross, where all Morris's undertakings were housed under one roof. The next ten years were to be the most prolific of all for Morris as a designer; among the many memorable works dating from this time are the *Clouds* and *Bullerswood* carpets, the great tapestries like *The Forest* and *The Orchard*, as well as the much-loved chintzes such as *Honeysuckle* and *Strawberry Thief*.

Vine and Acanthus *tapestry, designed and woven by Morris, 1879*

By 1875 Morris's reputation as a designer was firmly established, and it was a measure of the Firm's success that by now it had outlived the form in which it was originally constituted. There was some feeling among the partners that Morris tended to be high-handed; but to the majority of them work for the Firm had for some years been no more than a sideline – Burne-Jones, Webb and Morris had been virtually the only active members since 1870 – while to Morris the Firm was everything, providing him with an important source of income as well as satisfying his creativity and versatility and enabling him to put into practice his belief in the importance of art in everyday life.

When the time came for the Firm to be disbanded, Rossetti, Brown and Marshall caused some acrimony by demanding compensation – they finally received £100 each – but Burne-Jones, Webb and Faulkner waived any such claims. In 1875 the Firm was reorganized under Morris's sole direction, and henceforward would trade under the name of Morris and Co. A circular of 31 March 1875 announced this, stating that Burne-Jones and Webb, while no longer partners as before, would continue to provide designs for stained glass and furniture. Morris and Co. continued to be active right up until 1940, when the war made it impossible to maintain the standards originally set by William Morris, and the Company went into voluntary liquidation.

One of the most important moves made by Morris and Co. in its early days was the acquisition of showrooms at 449 Oxford Street, on the corner of North Audley Street (in 1917 the Company moved to 17 George Street, Hanover Square). The new showrooms provided a much more spacious and accessible showcase for the Company's goods than Queen Square, which continued as the works premises – indeed, it was at Queen Square that the first experiments were made in the weaving, dyeing and

Left: Morris and Co.'s showroom premises at 449 Oxford Street

Above: The Pond at Merton Abbey. *Watercolour and gouache, by I.I. Pocock*

fabric-printing for which Morris became so famous. Customers could now be received at Oxford Street in a much more satisfactory and appropriate way than had been possible at Queen Square, where Morris used to have to break off from work to see clients in the first floor office, still wearing his blue work clothes. More retail selling as well as commissioned work could be done at Oxford Street; curtains and upholstery were handled at 2B Granville Place nearby, and for furniture-making the Company later acquired the cabinet-makers Messrs. Holland's premises in Pimlico. Customers were invited to visit the works and see for themselves how Morris goods were made.

With the foundation of Morris and Co., several loyal members of staff became right-hand men to Morris, proving invaluable when more of their employer's time became taken up with lecturing on both design matters and the socialist beliefs to which he became increasingly committed, as well as all the design work he unremittingly continued to produce. George Wardle had replaced Warington Taylor as business manager after the latter's death in 1870, and he stayed with Morris for 20 years, until he was succeeded jointly by the brothers F. and R. Smith who had run the showroom. J. H. Dearle joined the Firm in 1873, working initially as an assistant in the showroom, then as a glass-painting apprentice, before moving on to tapestry weaving in which he was personally trained by Morris. Later Dearle became general manager of the Merton Abbey works, his responsibilities there increasing as Morris became deeply involved with the Kelmscott Press during the last years of his life (see Chapter 6). At this time, too, another right-hand man would be Sidney Cockerell, who was first invited by Morris to catalogue his personal library and went on to become his personal secretary and finally secretary to the Kelmscott Press.

Morris's London home for most of the Morris and Co. period, and for the rest of his life, was at Hammersmith, on Upper Mall. Originally called The Retreat, which Morris said reminded him of an asylum, it was renamed Kelmscott House after Kelmscott Manor, from which it was some 130 miles distant by river; Morris made the journey by water twice, on expeditions with family and friends, in 1880 and 1881. A special feature of the lovely Georgian house is the long drawing room running the entire width of the front, with river views from all its windows; the dining room at the back overlooks the long rambling garden which Morris loved, with its lawn, orchard and kitchen garden.

The 10 years following the establishment of Morris and Co. were the most prolific for Morris as a designer. Mackail, his biographer, credits him with over 600 designs for wallpapers, chintzes, woven fabrics, damasks, carpets, tapestries, rugs, stained glass and embroideries during this period.

Dyeing

Morris's researches and practical experiments in the use of natural dyes are among the most remarkable of his many achievements. He regarded dyeing as another of the endangered crafts he was seeking to revive, and gives a full account of the subject in his Arts and Crafts essay of 1889, 'Of Dyeing as an Art'. In fact he is so explicit in this essay that after reading it, as May Morris puts it, 'One could almost go to the dye-pots and start producing beautiful colours regardless of the years of experience needed to pursue this art.' Morris used his own dyes for the fabrics and rugs he produced, and thus it can be said that dyeing was crucial to the Company's output; in fact, towards the end of 1875, when Morris was hard at work perfecting techniques for his hand-printed chintzes, he wrote that if he did not achieve the results he was looking for with dyes, he would give up the production of textiles altogether.

Morris first became interested in dyeing at Queen Square when he was looking for the special shades required for silks and wools in embroidery work (see pages 103–7). What he wanted was naturally brilliant, fast yet soft colours, not the harsh, strident ones prevalent at the time, which were the result of commercial aniline dyes made from coal tar. These Morris rejected totally, not only for their lack of subtlety, but also for their unreliability, as with these dyes the original colours would change beyond recognition as they faded. In fact Morris regarded the invention of aniline dyes as the source of the divorce which had taken place between the commer-

Right: The Dining Room at Kelmscott House, Hammersmith, papered in Pimpernel, *from a photograph of the 1890s*

cial process and the original art of natural vegetable dyeing, which he set about reviving.

Since the use of vegetable dyes was obsolete, and there was nowhere Morris could observe it at first hand, he went right back to the grass roots, consulting French dyers' manuals, and finding that old herbals by Gerard, Matthiolus and Fuschsius proved valuable sources of information. May Morris recalls looking through Gerard's *Herbal* with her father, who obviously also found it a source of inspiration for pattern de

signs; for example, she mentions the *Lily* wallpaper design as strongly reminiscent of Gerard.

Morris's business manager, George Wardle, provided Morris with an invaluable contact for his dyeing researches. The Wardles were originally a family of silk dyers, and George's brother Thomas, who owned a works at Leek, in Staffordshire, printed many of Morris's chintzes in the period before the move to Merton Abbey. Morris made frequent visits to Leek in 1875–7 and corresponded profusely with

Thomas Wardle, who showed the results of his collaboration with Morris,
first on dyeing and then on printing
fabrics, in his exhibit at the 1878 Paris
Exposition Universelle. Morris devised
his own formulae for vegetable dyes,
and lists in fascinating detail the natural
sources for these in his Arts and Crafts
essay: blue from indigo and woad; red
from the insects kermes and cochineal
and the plant madder; yellow from weld,
poplar, osier, birch, broom and quer-
citron; brown from walnut tree roots.

Of all the forms of dyeing, the use of
indigo was the most demanding. The
technique of indigo discharge printing
was both laborious and time-consum-
ing, requiring three days' preparation
and extremely accurate, delicate handling, but it paid dividends in terms of the
rich effects produced. Morris used the
indigo vats at Leek for his experiments,
and wrote excited letters at the time
about his experiences there.

A description of the indigo discharge
process in one of Morris and Co.'s early
20th century catalogues gives a clear
idea of the complexity of the work
involved:

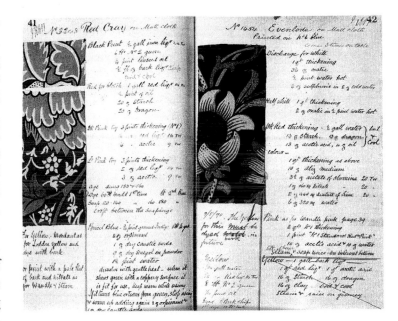

Above: *Pages from the Merton Abbey dye
book, 1882–91, with details on colourways
for the* Cray *and* Evenlode *chintzes*

Far left: *Morris's design for* Pimpernel
wallpaper, 1876

Left: Pimpernel *was the first of Morris's
wallpapers to feature the 'turnover' device*

*The cloth is first dyed all over in an
indigo vat to a uniform depth of blue,
and is then printed with a bleaching
reagent which either reduces or removes
the colour as required by the design.
Mordants are next printed on the
bleached parts and others where red is
wanted, and the whole length of the
material is then immersed in madder
vat calculated to give the proper tint.
This process is repeated for the yellow,*

*the three colours being superimposed on
each other to give green, purple and
orange. All loose colouring matter is
then cleared away and the colours are
set by passing the fabric through soap
at almost boiling heat.*

*The final treatment in the process is
to lay the cloth flat on the grass, with
its printed face to the light, so that the
whites in the designs may be completely
purified, and all fugitive colour
removed in nature's own way.*

Merton Abbey

The old larder at Queen Square was converted into a small dye-house, but this was only big enough to accommodate experiments, and much more spacious premises were needed for dyeing on a large scale. In 1881 Morris and Co. moved their works to Merton Abbey, near Morden in Surrey, set in idyllic surroundings on the River Wandle (after which one of Morris's richest and most beautiful chintzes was named), yet only seven miles from Charing Cross. Proximity to London was important – Morris had considered the Cotswold village of Blockley near Chipping Campden as a possible site but had had to turn the idea down as being too remote a place to be practical.

The premises at Merton Abbey had originally been a silk-weaving factory started in the early 18th century by Huguenot weavers, and were being used to print cheap tablecloths – about which Morris was very disparaging – when he took over. The works buildings were long and low-lying, not at all like the usual Victorian factory, with seven acres of grounds and a delightful cottage garden from which flowers would often be given to visitors to take back to town. The River Wandle, teeming with trout, provided pure water perfect for dyeing purposes – William de Morgan, who set up a ceramics works nearby, later moving to Chelsea from where he continued to supply Morris and Co. with tiles, helped Morris bring away bottled samples of the Wandle water for testing, and it was found to contain special qualities ideal for madder-dyeing. The property was planted with willows and poplars for use in obtaining dyes, and the open buttercup meadows were ideal for stretching out lengths of freshly dyed fabric to dry.

Most importantly, Merton Abbey meant that all Morris and Co.'s enterprises could be gathered under one roof: besides the indigo vats, there was a special dye-house for chintzes, and another for silk and wool. The looms for weaving the carpets which Morris had added to his repertoire by the early 1880s (see page 107) were housed on the ground floor, with the block printing shop above.

Visitors to Merton Abbey often remarked on the light, airy premises, and the peace and beauty of the rural

Above: Printing chintzes in the Morris and Co. workshops at Merton Abbey

Right: The Morning Room, Standen, near East Grinstead, Sussex, showing curtains and wall hangings of Daffodil chintz

setting. What Morris achieved here was indeed the Ruskinian ideal of production in the most pleasant of surroundings and working conditions. Morris featured Merton in his lecture 'A Factory as it Might Be' and his manager, George Wardle, who with Morris closely supervised all the work at Merton Abbey, summed it up perfectly when he said. 'There is nothing to say except that it was altogether delightful.'

Chintzes

Morris's remarkable achievements in obtaining subtle, rich and fast colours by means of his own vegetable dyes and the perfection of the indigo discharge technique, were crucial to the success of the beautiful hand-printed cotton fabrics for which he is probably most famous today. It is as though the motifs taken from nature, the flowers, trees, leaves and fruit, which Morris used to such superb effect in his pattern designs, were thematically reinforced by the use of the vegetable dyes: as W. R. Lethaby put it in his chapter on Morris in his memoir *Philip Webb and His Work*, it is 'as if the cloths were stained through and through with the juices of flowers'.

Morris chintzes were personalized by means of the hand-printing process in a way that could never be achieved by the use of mechanical engraved rollers, and were diversified and varied to extraordinary effect by the use of different colourways. Unlike Morris and Co.'s

more costly woven fabrics, embroideries, tapestries and hand-tufted rugs, these chintzes were within the means of the average middle-class household, and could be used effectively in even the smallest quantity: cushion covers or a small upholstered chair, for example, could add a special touch to the overall look of a room. Affordability must have contributed a great deal to the success of the chintzes which became one of Morris's hallmarks. It is significant that although Morris originally designed chintzes for use in large expanses as wall hangings, this has probably been their least frequent use, although a room like the Morning Room at Standen, for example, which is hung with the *Daffodil* chintz, gives a very good idea of how attractive the material could look used in this way.

Morris's early attempts to produce hand-printed cottons had not been successful. The somewhat naive *Jasmine Trail* or *Trellis* (c. 1868–70), and *Tulip and Willow* (1873) were not satisfactory to Morris when they were printed for him by the Lancashire printer Thomas Clarkson at the Bannister Hall Print Works, Preston. However, Morris's meeting with Thomas Wardle and their subsequent successful collaboration in natural dyeing processes, led to Wardle handling the printing of Morris and Co.'s fabrics before the move to Merton Abbey made it possible for this to be done on their own premises. The connection with Wardle meant that Morris

From the left: *Working drawing and block for* Kennet *printed cotton, 1883 (right).* Kennet *was also available in velveteen and woven silk*

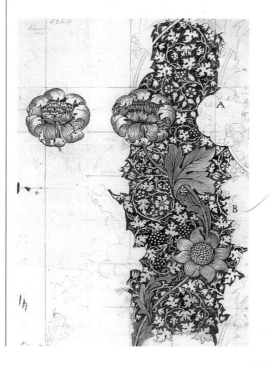

could now successfully revive his interest in hand-printed fabrics and indulge it to the full. Of the nearly 40 chintz designs which he produced, over half are dated between 1876 and 1883.

In March 1882 Morris was interviewed extensively by the Examiners to the Royal Commission on Technical Instruction on his views on design and his achievements as a designer. The discussion was wide-ranging, touching on many subjects lying at the heart of Morris's design ethic, and it is a valuable source of information on Morris's approach to design and the decorative arts generally. One of the topics on which he was questioned was what he felt could be done to counter the flood of textile designs from France with which English designers found themselves in competition at this time. Morris described a recent visit he had made to the works of

a Manchester calico printer who imported most of his designs from France, and made it clear that he had no time for these French designs, which he felt lacked originality and the sense of line and colour natural to the English.

Morris's own contribution in practical terms to counteracting the mass-production of cheap cottons in the Lancashire mills, in designs which he considered derivative and worthless, began with the *Tulip* in 1875, printed by Thomas Wardle and the first chintz to be commercially produced by Morris

Below left: *In the* African Marigold *chintz, 1876, Morris used the vertical turnover structure*

Below right: *The turnover pattern again in the* Brother Rabbit *chintz, 1882*

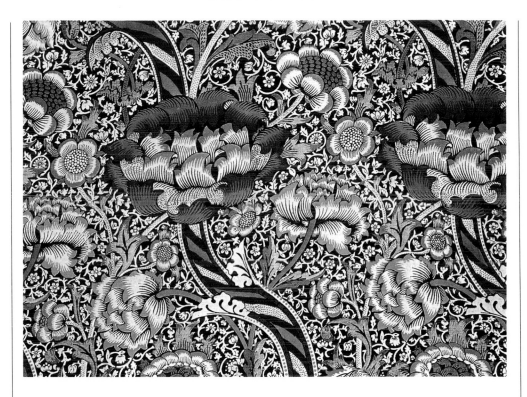

Above: The Wandle *chintz, 1884. The strong diagonal emphasis is characteristic of this period*

and Co. This was quickly followed next year by May Morris's personal favourite, the *Honeysuckle*, which she described as 'the most truly "Morrisian" in character of all his pattern-making in mid-life'. The pattern, with its honeysuckle, fritillaries and gorgeous poppies whose leaves form an inner net set against a background of yew twigs, is organized around a 'turnover' structure which was most probably derived from Morris's particular interest in weaving at this time (see page 95). Other outstanding examples of designs in which the pattern turns over mirror-wise around a verti-cal axis, all dated 1876–7 and all printed by Thomas Wardle at Leek, are *African Marigold* (see opposite page), *Iris*, *Columbine/Bluebell* (see page 15), *Snake's-head* (see page 26) and *Little Chintz*.

After the move to Merton Abbey in 1881, when for the first time in the history of Morris and Co. both dyeing and hand-printing could be done on the same premises, under Morris's close personal supervision, he began to produce a steady stream of stunning chintzes: *Rose and Thistle*, *Brother Rabbit* and *Bird and Anemone*, all 1882, were among the first. *Brother Rabbit*, inspired by *Uncle Remus*, which was being read with great enjoyment at Kelmscott Manor around this time, is an example of a relatively simple use of the indigo discharge method: by using a weaker bleaching reagent, a half-tone effect was produced. The design, with its pairs of small animals and birds, still conforms to a marked turnover pattern. *Bird and Anemone*, which was issued as both a wallpaper and chintz – the exception rather than the rule with Morris, as already noted – was another personal favourite of May Morris, with its cleverly masked repeat pattern of 'crisply fluttering birds'. A stronger solution of bleaching reagent was used in this case, to take out the indigo dye completely, leaving a white area. Birds featured again the following year in one of Morris's best-loved chintz designs, the *Strawberry Thief*, which was inspired by Morris's observations of the thrushes under the strawberry nets at Kelmscott Manor. May Morris loved the design, which she described as 'a very flower garden for colour', adding endearingly, 'the livestock is adorable', and she conjures up the following delightfully vivid scene:

You can picture my Father going out in the early morning and watching the rascally thrushes at work on the fruit-beds and telling the gardener who growls, 'I'd like to wring their necks!' that no bird in the garden must be touched. There were certainly more birds than strawberries in spite of attempts at protection. And the walls of the little dining-room are hung with this note of the June garden and the little lords of it.

Two small repeat pattern designs of this year, the *Eyebright* and *Flowerpot*, are of interest for both being lining fabrics,

but the most exciting development in Morris's designs for printed cottons, which manifested itself in 1883, was a new tendency towards a marked diagonal arrangement. Just as his earlier use of the vertical turnover structure has been seen to derive from his interest in weaving, the diagonal emphasis seems certainly to have been inspired by a 15th century Italian cut velvet acquired by the South Kensington Museum that year. From 1876 Morris had acted as assessor of students' work in the Museum's School of Design, and until the end of his life was frequently consulted by the Museum about purchases of textiles, carpets, books and manuscripts for their historic collections. In the Royal Commission on Technical Instruction's Examination referred to earlier, Morris said of the Museum's fine textile collection, 'Perhaps I have used it as much as any man living', pointing out that in his view a designer is 'bound to study old examples', which he is also 'bound to supplement . . . by a careful study of nature'. Nowhere is this combination of inspirational sources better seen than in the rivers sequence of chintzes including the *Kennet*, *Wey*, *Evenlode* and *Windrush* (all 1883), followed in 1884 by the *Wandle*, which May Morris claimed as 'literally the most "splendid" of Morris's designs', and the *Cray* (1884) and the *Cherwell*

Right: The Eyebright *printed cotton of 1883, like the* Flowerpot *of the same year, was designed specifically for use as a lining fabric*

(1887), all named for tributaries of the Thames, the river which meant so much to Morris. Others in his rivers series were the *Medway* and the *Lea* (both 1885), the *Avon* (1886), the *Trent* (1889) and the *Severn* (1890).

The outstanding feature of the diagonally biased designs was a distinctive continuous plant stem with offshoots making up a broken horizontal. In later chintzes of 1890–6 there is a move towards an upward, flowing movement, with a return to less rigid patterns, which seem to sway from side to side: this is particularly marked in the *Daffodil* chintz of 1891.

Wallpapers

Similar design trends can be discerned in the wallpapers produced by Morris and Co. A number of the 11 papers designed between 1876 and 1883 are characterized by an emphatic vertical turnover structure: the *Sunflower* and *Acorn* papers, both 1879, are particularly fine examples of this. Some 10 years later, striking examples of the predilection for diagonal movement which was still continuing to preoccupy Morris are the *Bruges* paper of 1888, described by May Morris as a '*tour de force* in the matter of skilful space-filling', and the *Norwich* paper the

following year. In 1890 the gorgeous *Pink and Rose* wallpaper illustrates superbly Morris's return to upward movement. *Blackthorn* (1892) is an especially good example of the bower-like effect Morris knew so well how to create by symmetrically building up the naturalistic elements of his designs, in this case daisies, fritillaries and blackthorn sprays, which also show a return to a degree of naturalism in plant forms which he had not used extensively since the late 1870s. *Spring Thicket* (1894) has a strongly marked net pattern similar to *Lily and Pomegranate* (1886). *Compton* (1896) marks a final return to less structured patterning, the flowers being scattered, rather than formally arranged, between the meanders. As previously mentioned, the *Compton* was issued as a chintz as well as a wallpaper; such a dual-purpose design meant that Morris's customers could have walls, drapes and upholstery all presented in the same pattern, if they chose. However, it is interesting to note just how effective the combination of different Morris designs for fabrics and wallpapers can also look in a single room: in one of the bedrooms at Standen, for example, the *Tulip* chintz

Above: The Flower Garden *woven silk designed by Morris in 1879 was also reproduced in woven silk and wool*

Far left: The Sunflower *wallpaper (1879) has a rigid vertical turnover pattern which is in marked contrast with the flowing design of* Willow Bough *(1887), left*

curtains hang most felicitously against the *Willow-bough* wallpaper. The timeless quality of the designs for both wallpapers and fabrics is quite extraordinary, and today they look equally good in traditional or modern settings.

Woven textiles

Weaving was one of the first crafts to suffer from mass industrialization, and so reviving the obsolete art of handweaving was especially close to Morris's heart, as is apparent, for example, in his lecture on the subject in 'The Lesser Arts of Life', published in 1882.

Five years previously, in a letter dated 25 March 1877, Morris had written to Thomas Wardle in Leek asking him for advice in obtaining the services of a Frenchman from the world-famous silk-weaving centre at Lyons. A Monsieur Bazin was subsequently employed to erect Morris and Co.'s first Jacquard silk loom at 26 Queen Square and to advise on its use. One of the early silks woven on the hand loom at Queen Square was the *Willow*, adapted from the earlier wallpaper (see page 73) and known in at least six colourways. The *Flower Garden* silk of 1879, also woven at Queen Square, came in two especially beautiful colourways, a red and tawny buff, and a green and gold.

Below: St James, *woven silk damask, 1881, available in six colourways*

Weaving at Queen Square was obviously necessarily limited, and it was not until the move to Merton Abbey that the full potential of the weaving side of Morris's business could be fully realized. In fact, before this some of Morris's designs had to be woven on power looms: for example, J. O. Nicholson of Macclesfield wove the *Oak* and *St James* silk damasks, both registered in 1881, on the power loom for Morris and Co., although both silks were later hand-woven at Merton Abbey. The *Oak* was available in numerous colours, shot blue and green being much in demand, though it was among the most expensive of Morris fabrics at 45s per yard. May Morris tells how her mother had a dress made of the green version, with its

'moon-beam lights', 'fit only for her stately figure' — Morris silks were not generally popular with dressmakers, who found the superfine fabric difficult to work with.

The *St James* silk was designed as part of the commission to refurbish the Throne and Reception Rooms at St James's Palace, described on page 75; it was suitably majestic in crimson and gold, but was also available to order in four alternative colourways.

Experiments were made in weaving velvets but were dropped when the results proved prohibitively expensive. Only the *Granada* of 1884, with a cut silk pile in three colours, brocaded in gold thread, was produced, in small quantity, at an amazing £10 per yard.

Much more practical and remarkably hard-wearing were Morris's woven wool fabrics, which could be used for curtains, wall hangings or upholstery. The woven woollen double cloth, *Bird* (1878), first woven at Queen Square and later at Merton Abbey, was extremely popular with customers and indeed with Morris himself. The *Peacock and Dragon*, another heavy compound-weave wool, belongs to this same year; two splendid pairs of curtains in this fabric hang in the Tapestry Room at Kelmscott Manor. Like both the *Bird* and the *Peacock and Dragon*, the popular *Bird and Vine*

Below: Granada, *woven silk velvet brocaded with gilt thread, 1884*

(1879) follows the repeat turnover pattern Morris liked so much, and which he adapted from medieval Spanish and Sicilian woven textiles. He used the same device to great effect in *Dove and Rose* the same year; this fabric combined wool with silk, a combination of which Morris was particularly fond, to create interesting textural effects: *Dove and Rose* was used in the magnificent drawing room at Wightwick Manor, the house at Wolverhampton which Morris decorated for the wealthy Birmingham industrialist Theodore Mander (see page 113). In fact two Morris designs had been woven three years previously in silk and wool, the *Anemone* and the *Honeycomb* (later used as a carpet design), both power-loom woven by H. C. McCrea. The *Tulip and Rose*, also 1876 and also used for carpeting, was woven in silk and linen by the Heckmondwike Manufacturing Company.

Once Morris and Co. moved to Merton Abbey, Morris was able to produce an extensive range of handwoven fabrics, and he employed a number of former Spitalfields weavers to handle the work, giving them the chance to revive skills which industrialization had rendered defunct. May Morris gives a touching description of these workers: 'It was always somewhat pathetic to watch the weavers at work here at their handlooms — old men from Spitalfields who had been prosperous once and had been through bad times, saddened by the changes in industrial life that with its scurry and thrusting aside, had passed them by.'

Tapestry

As mentioned earlier, Morris's early embroideries had been designed to look like tapestry, which he regarded as the 'noblest of the weaving arts', the ideal corporate creative responsibility. While still an undergraduate, Morris had been impressed by the medieval tapestries he saw in the Cluny Museum in Paris. He always admired medieval as opposed to Renaissance tapestry work and intensely disliked the Gobelins tapestries with their lifeless, uncreative imitation of oil painting, a view which is reminiscent of the way he felt about stained glass. Indeed, analogies are drawn between tapestry and stained glass in an important Arts and Crafts essay by Morris on 'Textiles', published in 1893, where he describes tapestry, like stained glass, in terms of a 'mosaic of pieces of colour', adding that good tapestry work should contain 'plenty of crisp detail' in the same way as stained glass.

In everything Morris wrote about weaving and tapestry, he was speaking from first-hand experience, because, as in all his work, he learnt the techniques for himself, which undoubtedly was one of his great strengths as a designer. In the Examination by the Royal Commission on Technical Instruction, he had reinforced his important point that 'it is desirable that the artist and what is technically called the designer should practically be one' by adding, 'A designer ought to be able to weave himself.' He certainly put this into practice on his own account, teaching himself the art of tapestry from a pre-Revol-

ution French Arts et Métiers (arts and crafts) handbook, just as he had turned to early French handbooks for guidance when he was experimenting with dyeing. He totally rejected low-warp loom weaving on the grounds that it was almost entirely mechanical, as the weaver had to work from the back of the tapestry, looking down through the threads at the design below. With the high-warp loom, on the other hand, the weaver's position was more like that of an artist at his easel.

Above: In the Flora *(left) and* Pomona *(right) tapestries, 1885, Burne-Jones designed the figures, Morris the backgrounds*

Morris installed a high-warp loom in his bedroom at Kelmscott House and kept diary notes of his weaving times and progress, usually setting to work between 5 and 6 in the morning to fit in several hours' weaving before turning to all the other things he had to do. A diary entry towards the end of May 1881

gives a good idea of just how busy his life was at this time: 'Up at 5: $3\frac{1}{2}$ hours tapestry. To Grange. To Queen Square: The green for Peacock all wrong. Did day books and Friday . . . took away model of G. H. carpet from K. Meeting St Mark's Committee. Dined A. Ionides.'

The first tapestry Morris wove, in wool on a cotton warp, was the brilliantly instinctive *Vine and Acanthus* (1879), which he liked to call the *Cabbage and Vine*; he noted a total of 516 hours' weaving time for this piece over a four-month period, and as May Morris put it, 'The whole piece might be the work of a craftsman with years of training behind him.' This tapestry now hangs in the Screens Passage on the ground floor at Kelmscott Manor, and the original design is in the Victoria and Albert Museum.

This was the only full-size piece of tapestry Morris designed and wove in its entirety, but another remarkable piece of which he was the sole designer is the *Woodpecker* (1885), woven in wool and silk on cotton warp (see page 11). The design of the bird perched in a tree and garlanded with flowers, fruits and swirling leaves incorporates a border with an embroidered inscription of Morris's own verse which, like all his poetry featured in tapestry work, would be included as 'Verses for Pictures' in the collection *Poems By the Way*. The same device is used in the *Pomona* and *Flora* pair of tapestries of 1885, also woven in wool and silk on cotton warp. The figures for both these tapestries were designed by Burne-Jones, and the backgrounds by Morris. The black-letter verse at the top and the foot of the *Pomona* panel reads:

sit and see. nor ride nor haste

and Co. tapestries were most often combined efforts. The figure designs tended to be by Burne-Jones, with Philip Webb providing the animals and birds, and Morris and J. H. Dearle the backgrounds. Dearle, who had been taught tapestry-weaving by Morris himself, in turn taught two apprentices, Sleath and Knight, who worked on both the *Flora* and the *Pomona*. Later, following the typical Morris and Co. recruitment practice, the Merton Abbey housekeeper's nephew was employed to work on a third high-warp loom.

Especially famous Morris and Co. tapestries include the *Goose Girl* (1883), designed by Walter Crane and worked on by Dearle. The *Forest* (1887) was commissioned by Alexander Ionides for his house at 1 Holland Park (see page 112), with animals by Webb, foliage by Morris and a floral ground by Dearle. The *Orchard* (1890) was unusual in that Morris designed the figures, as well as the fruit trees (Dearle again supplied the floral ground); the figure design was adapted by Morris from cartoons for angels done for the nave roof at Jesus College chapel, Cambridge. Both the *Forest* and the *Orchard* are now in the Victoria and Albert Museum.

I am the ancient apple queen:
As once I was so am I now,
For evermore a hope unseen,
Betwixt the blossom and the bough.
Ah, where's the river's hidden gold —
And where the windy grave of Troy —
Yet come I as I came of old,
From out the heart of summer's gold.

This is echoed on the companion *Flora* with:

I am the handmaid of the earth
I broider fair her glorious gown,
And deck her on her days of mirth
With many a garland of renown.
And while earth's little ones are fain
And play about the mother's hem,
I scatter every gift I gain
From sun and wind to gladden them.

Like their stained glass work, Morris

Above left: *The* Forest *tapestry, designed by Morris, 1887, with animals by Philip Webb*

Right: *Philip Webb's pencil drawing for the fox in* The Forest *tapestry*

Above: The magnificent Orchard tapestry, 1890, designed by Morris, with figures by Burne-Jones

Left: Morris's design for the foliage background of a tapestry, leaving the figure to be completed by other artists

Morris had been made an Honorary Fellow of Exeter College, Oxford, in 1883, and seven years later he and Burne-Jones jointly presented their old college with their *Adoration of the Magi* tapestry (sometimes known as the *Star of Bethlehem*), which can be seen today in the chapel. Sidney Cockerell records Morris as saying of this tapestry, 'nothing better of the kind had been done, old or new', and his pride in his work was well founded: this proved the most popular of all the Merton Abbey tapestries and a number of subsequent repeats were sold, including one to Eton College, for their chapel.

The culmination of Morris and Co.'s tapestry work undoubtedly came, however, with the six *San Graal* narrative panels, woven for William Knox d'Arcy, an Australian mining engineer 'of advanced tastes', as May Morris nicely put it, for the dining room at Stanmore Hall, the house designed for him by Philip Webb. Burne-Jones began his designs for the Holy Grail cycle in 1890–91, and the work was executed in 1891–4. The subjects of the panels were: 1) The Knights of the Round Table summoned to the Quest by the Strange Damsel. 2) The Arming and Departure of the Knights. 3) The Failure of Sir Launcelot to enter the Chapel of the Holy Grail. 4) The Failure of Sir Gawaine. 5) The Ship. 6) The Attainment. Another complete set was done for Mr McCulloch, William d'Arcy's partner, for his house in Queen's Gate, London, and partial repeats were made for other clients, including Laurence Hodson of Compton Hall.

Embroideries

As seen in Chapters 2 and 3, embroidery was an early interest of Morris: he had taught himself the craft while living in Red Lion Square before his marriage, and embroideries, both ecclesiastical and domestic, were an important part of the Firm's output right from the beginning. As well as specially commissioned finished embroideries, very popular for wall hangings, Morris would also supply designs and materials to clients for them to work at home. Morris and Burne-

Jones designed a five-panel frieze on the theme of Chaucer's *Romaunt de la Rose* for the dining room of Rounton Grange, Northallerton, Yorkshire, designed by Webb for the Yorkshire industrialist Sir Lowthian Bell in 1872–6; Lady (Margaret) Bell and her daughter Florence Johnson worked the frieze in wools, silk and gold thread on linen.

The Bells' other daughter, Ada, shared her mother's and sister's considerable skill, and when she married Major Godman and went to live at Smeaton Manor, also near Northallerton and also designed by Webb, she commissioned from Morris a design for wall hangings that was to prove extremely popular. This was the *Artichoke* panel, which Ada Godman executed in crewel work on twilled linen, using wools in beautiful gradated shades of

Below: A detail from The Attainment, *one of the six panels of the* San Graal *sequence of tapestries*

blue, with soft greens and several shades of brown, the flower-heads tipped with carmine. The same design was worked in silks by Mrs Margaret Beale, another fine needlewoman, and her daughters for Standen, the house near East Grinstead designed for the solicitor J. S. Beale by Webb. Another embroidery worked by Mrs Beale, to Morris's *Vine* design, can be seen hanging in the Hall at Standen.

Embroidery kits on a less grand scale, which could double as cushion covers or fire screens, were always valuable money-spinners for Morris and Co. Designs for these included the *Flower-pot*, *Rosewreath* and *Rosebush*, *Olive and Rose*, *Apple Tree* and *Clanfield*. Coverlets and portières were always popular, and Catherine Holiday, wife of the painter and stained glass designer Henry Holiday, specialized in designs for these, as well as supplying Morris with finished articles; she also sold work independently to the United States. Other popular embroidered items on sale in the Oxford Street shop were evening bags, workbags, gloves, nightdress cases, bell pulls, tea cosies, book covers, photograph frames, tablecloths and billiard table covers.

May Morris

Morris was a regular visitor and adviser to the Royal School of Art Needlework (founded in 1872) who used a number of his designs, some of which they featured in their exhibit at the Philadelphia Centennial Exhibition in 1876. In 1885 he handed over Morris and Co.'s embroidery department to his daughter May, who after studying at the South Kensington School of Design had been working for the Company for an initial three-year period. May, who as already seen possessed a strong instinctive insight into her father's attitudes towards his work, was herself a highly talented embroideress and designer.

Like her father, May's approach to the craft of embroidery – which she elevated from the status of minor pastime to art form in its own right – was founded on a belief in the importance of good design, based on a complete practical knowledge of the techniques and materials of the craft. Like her father, too, she felt that all the decorative arts

Below: Flowerpot, designed by Morris, c. 1880 and embroidered by May Morris

should aim to make best use of materials specially natural to them, 'to achieve something that could not be done with any other', as Morris put it in his 1881 lecture, 'Art and the Beauty of the Earth'. For this reason, May disliked the type of embroidery represented by Berlin woolwork – very popular in the early 19th century – because it was not only harsh of hue but derivative, imitative of painting.

May Morris exhibited widely and taught and lectured on embroidery as well as acting as an embroidery consultant. She lectured in the United States in 1909–10, and an exhibition of her work in New York was arranged to coincide with this. Her book for beginners, *Decorative Needlework*, was published in 1893. She did much to champion the cause of women as artists in their own right, and she was a founder of the Women's Guild of Arts in 1907.

At Morris and Co. May headed a team of embroideresses, Fanny Wright, Maud Deacon, Ellen Wright and Lily Yeats (sister of the poet), working from her own premises near her parents' house, at 8 Hammersmith Terrace, following her marriage to Hilary Sparling. Among her finest embroidery designs are the *Orchard* or *Fruit Garden* portière (c. 1892) and the *June* frieze and *Battye* wall hanging (both c. 1900). The *Orchard* is worked in silks on Morris's *Oak* silk damask, this base fabric playing an important part in the composition as a whole, which consists of slender-trunked fruit trees with swirling foliage against a background of acanthus leaves and flowers.

Above: Bedcover designed by William Morris, c. 1876, and worked in silks on linen by Catherine Holiday

The *Battye* wall hanging

The *Battye* wall hanging, one of May Morris's most ambitious designs, differs from the *Orchard* in that the whole surface of the loose-woven canvas is worked over in silks. The piece was commissioned by Mrs Battye and worked by her; it is likely that the colours of the silks, chosen to create a remarkable iridescent, softly shimmering effect, were personally selected by May for her client's use. Woodland trees supporting shields bearing the

The.tre.rem'dynan'ðat Countie for you'
not.ye.honde.ye.planted.itt. croppes till June is passe

Jyne.try
-eth.trothe

deoill.take.

ye.hyndemost

de Noe.manne.ys.a.prophet.inne Pennye.wyse:
ne hys.owne.countrie pounde.foolyshe.

Battye family heraldic arms feature in this wall hanging. The wood is alive with birds – ravens, doves, an owl, a robin, a heron with a fish in its beak – and small animals, a squirrel and a rabbit, complete the picture, which is framed in vertical borders of oak leaves and acorns.

A delightful feature of the hanging is the humorous mottoes contained in scrolls, for example: 'Bear and forbeare'; 'Wyne inne, wytte oute'; 'Face the sonne but turne youre backke to the storme'; 'The earlic birde getteth the wurme'; 'The lyvynge dogge is more thanne the dede lyonne'; 'Penny wyse: pounde foolyshe', etc.

The *June* frieze, worked in wools on linen, is of special interest for its inscription, the middle verse of the poem 'June' from Morris's *Earthly Paradise*, and for the depiction of Kelmscott Manor in a central panel. Verse features again, this time specially composed by Morris, 'For the bed at Kelmscott', on the valance for the 17th century oak four-poster which can be seen in William Morris's bedroom at Kelmscott Manor. This and the pair of bed curtains – reminiscent, in the background design, of the *Trellis* wallpaper – were designed by May and worked by her and other members of her embroidery team. Her mother embroidered the coverlet, signing it 'Si je puis. Jane Morris. Kelmscott'.

Left: *The* Battye *hanging, designed by May Morris c. 1900, was worked in silks on canvas by members of the Battye family*

Carpets

These complete the full range of Morris's output: in an exhibition in 1880 Morris and Co. were able to show no fewer than 24 carpet designs. In the circular issued by the company for the exhibition, Morris wrote: '. . . the art of Carpet-making, in common with the rather special arts of the East, is either dead or dying fast . . . we people of the West must make our own hand-made Carpets . . . and these, while they should equal the Eastern ones as nearly as may be in materials and durability, should by no means imitate them in design, but show themselves obviously to be the outcome of modern and Western ideas, guided by those principles that underlie all architectural art in common' – yet another resounding statement of his artistic beliefs practically applied to another of the decorative arts which he worked so hard to revive.

In fact Morris's first designs were for Kidderminster, Wilton and Axminster machine-made carpets, usually woven by the Heckmondwike Manufacturing Company or the Wilton Carpet Works, most often in blue/green. Especially popular designs, produced between 1875 and 1880, were the *Daisy* or *Grass*, the *Artichoke*, the *Lily*, *Rose*, *Tulip*, and *Lily* and *Bellflowers*. A choice of borders, depending on where in the house the carpet was to be laid, was always available.

It was a natural progression for Morris to move on to hand-knotted carpets and rugs, and experiments with these were made first, as for tapestry, at

Above: Tulip and Lily *design by Morris, c. 1875, for Kidderminster carpeting*

Queen Square, where a carpet knotter from Glasgow was specially employed to teach nimble-fingered girls how to do the work. Carpet weaving was then done at separate premises in the former coach-house at Hammersmith, and finally at Merton Abbey.

The carpets and rugs produced at Hammersmith, and so-called for their place of origination, were distinguished by the device of the hammer, large 'M' and wavy line representing the river, woven into the border. Morris designed almost all Morris and Co.'s carpets himself, making a carefully coloured drawing about one-eighth of the full size

of the design, which was then enlarged by a draughtsman on to squared point paper, each point representing a single knot. Morris and Co. did all their own pointing, at Morris's insistence, after an early disaster with a Kidderminster design of Morris's: the sample produced was unrecognizable through faulty drawing by the manufacturer's designer.

In his Arts and Crafts 'Textiles' essay of 1889 Morris makes an interesting distinction between the specific use of design motifs and colour contrast in carpets and other types of weaving: carpet designs should be quite elementary in form, because of the comparative coarseness of the medium, and the motifs should be merely suggestive of natural forms such as foliage, flowers, birds and animals, rather than attempting to depict them in detail; colours should be juxtaposed rather than graded as in tapestry.

Hammersmith carpets were highly expensive, but in great demand by Morris's wealthy clients. At Stanmore Hall, for example, large carpets were made for both drawing rooms, the dining room, library and vestibule. The *Clouds* carpet commissioned by Percy Wyndham (see page 113) was enormous — 12 × 3.76 metres (39 × 12¼ feet) — and the *Naworth* carpet for George Howard (the 'G. H. carpet' referred to in the diary extract quoted on page 100) took a year to weave on the big carpet frame at Merton Abbey. The *Bullerswood* carpet, made for the Sandersons' home at Chislehurst, Kent, which was shown at the 1893 Arts and Crafts Exhibition, and is now in the Victoria and Albert Museum, had 25 Ghiordes knots to the square inch. The smaller, coarser, deep-pile rugs were of course less prohibitively expensive: a particularly lovely wool pile on cotton warps, now also in the Victoria and Albert Museum, was made around 1888 for Mrs Mackail, wife of Morris's biographer.

The influence of Morris and Co.

By the early 1880s Morris products were a household word and Morris's reputation was established as far afield as the United States. Most middle-class households included some Morris design as part of their decoration; many, especially in Norman Shaw's London garden suburb of Bedford Park (1878), for example, made a point of decorating with Morris throughout, illustrating William Morris's own belief that even the most modest home could be made beautiful provided everything in it was well designed and above all useful. As he put it in his 'Lesser Arts' lecture to the Trades Guild of Learning in 1877, 'nothing can be a work of art which is not useful . . .' and again in 'The Beauty of Life' lecture in 1880, 'Have nothing in your homes which you do not know to be useful or believe to be beautiful'.

Below: The Drawing Room at Clouds, featuring the specially commissioned carpet

Morris's refreshingly down-to-earth approach is well illustrated in this second lecture: here, the man who furnished some of the grandest homes for some of Britain's wealthiest men (see page 111), gives a description of an ideal living room which would not be out of place in a Habitat catalogue today:

First a book-case with a great many books in it: next a table that will keep steady when you write or work at it; then several chairs that you can move, and a bench that you can sit or lie upon; next a cupboard with drawers . . . you will want pictures or engravings, such as you can afford, only not stopgaps, but real works of art on the wall; or else the wall itself must be ornamented with some beautiful and restful pattern . . . a vase or two to put flowers in, which latter you must have sometimes, if you live in a town. Then there will be the fireplace of course, which in our climate is bound to be the chief object in a room . . . a small carpet which can be bundled out of the room in 2 minutes, will be useful.

Morris's views on interior decoration reached a wide audience through the national and international exhibitions in which he frequently showed his products. In 1883, for example, he exhibited at the Boston Foreign Fair, and the brochure Morris and Co. produced for this event gives many interesting insights into how Morris thought his goods could best be used, with practical advice on such matters as the choice of

Above: *Watercolour design for* Redcar *carpet, a Hammersmith wool on cotton warp rug, designed by Morris in the 1880s. The finished carpet is opposite*

the right pattern of wallpaper according to the function it is to fulfil, or the introduction of points of colour into a room through the strategic use of upholstered chairs and sofas, which do not need to be uniform in colour or design. He also emphasizes his familiar love of white paintwork, and his preference for fabric wall hangings and coverings.

At home, Morris and Co. were well represented at the Arts and Crafts exhibitions. The Art Workers' Guild had been established in 1884, and the Arts and Crafts Exhibition Society evolved from it three years later. The Society was formed in reaction against

the Royal Academy of Arts' rigid, unprogressive adherence to painting, sculpture and 'abstract' architecture, to the exclusion of the decorative arts. Its purpose was to organize public exhibitions of work in these 'lesser arts', and to accompany the exhibitions with public lectures. Morris, who was a member of the executive committee, contributed a number of stimulating lectures and papers to the scheme, which were published in the Arts and Crafts Exhibition catalogues; at the first exhibition held at the New Gallery in the autumn of 1888 Morris and Co. showed high-warp tapestries, silks, chintzes and hand-made carpets. Widely published in such art periodicals as the *Studio* at home and *Der Moderne Stil* abroad, Morris came to exert a very wide-reaching influence on good taste, and designers like Charles Ricketts, Charles Shannon, George Walton and Hugh Baillie Scott would feature his designs in their interiors.

Morris houses

Some of the houses designed by Philip Webb, for which Morris provided the interior decoration, have already been referred to in this review of the various products and services supplied by

Above: *The Billiard Room, Wightwick Manor, wallpaper:* Pimpernel: *curtains:* Bird; *sofa:* Tulip and Rose; *carpet:* Tulip and Lily

Morris and Co. The Webb/Morris partnership was ideally complementary in every way, and never more so than over the commission at 1 Holland Park, executed in the 1880s for Alexander Ionides, a wealthy cotton importer of Greek extraction. This was indeed 'an epoch-making house', as Gleeson White's article of 1898 in the *Studio* was entitled, and the estimates and bills for the job, now in the Victoria and Albert Museum, make fascinating reading. Mr Ionides was clearly very satisfied, for

Webb and Morris went on to execute a commission from a friend of his, J.S. Beale – this was Standen, near East Grinstead, which was designed as the Beales' country home. This charming house, set in a lovely garden with superb views over the River Medway, contains many original pieces of furniture, carpets and embroideries, all of which can be seen by the public thanks to the National Trust.

Another important joint commission, in the 1880s, was Clouds, at East Knoyle, near Salisbury. This was built to Webb's design in 1883–6 and furnished throughout by Morris. It was burnt down in 1888–9, but rose phoenix-like from the ashes, again to Webb's design.

One of Morris's greatest achievements, however, was in a house designed not by Webb but by Edward Ould, in 1887–93. This was Wightwick Manor, near Wolverhampton, built for Theodore Mander, a wealthy paint and varnish manufacturer. Morris and Co. supplied all the wallpapers, curtains, upholstery, and rugs, as well as stained glass and tiles, and many further textiles were added by Sir Geoffrey and Lady Mander, who built up a magnificent collection of Pre-Raphaelite art. Lady Mander (Rosalie Grylls), who bequeathed Wightwick to the National Trust, wrote a remarkable article about the house as a William Morris period piece (published in *Connoisseur*, January 1962), in which she emphasizes the reaction Morris and Co.'s work represents against Victorian knick-knackery and mechanical mass-production.

Top right: *The splendid Oak Room at Wightwick Manor, near Wolverhampton*

Right: *Bill of 1887 from Morris and Co. to their client, Alexander Ionides*

THIS IS THE PICTURE OF THE OLD
HOUSE BY THE THAMES TO WHICH
THE PEOPLE OF THIS STORY WENT.
HEREAFTER FOLLOWS THE BOOK IT.
SELF WHICH IS CALLED NEWS FROM
NOWHERE OR AN EPOCH OF REST &
IS WRITTEN BY WILLIAM MORRIS.

NEWS FROM NOWHERE OR AN EPOCH OF REST.
CHAPTER I. DISCUSSION AND BED.

UP at the League, says a friend, there had been one night a brisk conversational discussion, as to what would happen on the Morrow of the Revolution, finally shading off into a vigorous statement by various friends, of their views on the future of the fully-developed new society.

SAYS our friend: Considering the subject, the discussion was good-tempered; for those present, being used to public meetings & after-lecture debates, if they did not listen to each other's opinions, which could scarcely be expected of them, at all events did not always attempt to speak all together, as is the custom of people in ordinary polite society when conversing

Chapter Six

THE KELMSCOTT PRESS (1890-6)

Although Morris had been a collector of early printed books and medieval manuscripts all his adult life and his talents for calligraphy and illumination had been revealed early on, he did not set up the Kelmscott Press until 1890. Printing was another craft in which standards had drastically declined, and with customary thoroughness Morris mastered all aspects of fine hand-printing, designing three typefaces, the 'Golden', the 'Troy' and the 'Chaucer'. Fifty-three books (a total of 18,234 volumes) were printed by the Press, including the Kelmscott *Chaucer*, one of the most elaborate books ever produced; it contained 87 woodcuts by Burne-Jones, a title-page, 14 borders, 18 frames and 26 decorated initials by Morris.

The frontispiece and opening page of News from Nowhere, *1892*

William Morris's interest in medieval illuminated manuscripts and early printed books manifested itself at an early date and continued throughout his life. As early as 1864 the poet Swinburne had introduced him to Frederick Startridge Ellis, who became a lifelong friend, publishing Morris's own writings and later sharing the tenancy of Kelmscott Manor with him, after the departure of Rossetti. In the year of their first meeting, Morris bought from Ellis the fine illustrated Ulm edition of Boccaccio's *Dream of Fair Women* (for £26). Over 30 years later, just a few weeks before his death, by which time he had assembled a collection of over 1,000 early printed books and manuscripts, as indicated by the 1890–1 catalogue of his library at Kelmscott House, Morris purchased for £1000 from the first Baron Aldenham a magnificent psalter which he named the Windmill psalter, after one of the illuminated miniatures it contained.

The founding of Morris's Kelmscott Press was a natural extension of this interest. Printing was another of the crafts which had suffered considerable commercial degradation, and which Morris sought to revive. As with the other decorative arts, he was not content just to design beautiful books, but went to considerable lengths to familiarize himself with all the materials and processes involved – the paper, ink, and the cutting and making of the type.

In the same way, Morris had not been content just to collect illuminated manuscripts – he had made his own. He was, as already seen in Chapter 2, an outstanding calligrapher and illuminator. In 1870, in collaboration with Burne-Jones and Charles Fairfax-Murray, who contributed miniatures, and George Wardle, who was responsible for other decorations, he had made a 51-page *Book of Verse*, a selection of his own lyric poems, as a birthday present for Georgiana Burne-Jones. Many of the exquisite floral and other decorative motifs used would recur in designs for wallpapers and fabrics. This jewel of a book must have been very well received, for two years later Morris gave Georgiana a beautifully illuminated version of the *Rubáiyát of Omar Khayyám*. Other examples of his work in this field were a manuscript of the odes of Horace, in 1875, and a translation of the *Aeneid*, in collaboration with Burne-Jones.

Morris's outstanding talent for calligraphy – he experimented with many types of penmanship – combined with his knowledge of block-printing, con-

tributed substantially to his success as a type designer. His authoritative Arts and Crafts essay on printing gives a survey of its early history and his own views on the principles of good typography, emphasizing the importance of legibility; well-designed and spaced type; well laid-out pages (stressing that the double, not the single, page should always be considered the unit), with margins in due proportion to the type area. Although Morris excelled at decorative borders and initials, he also felt that books could be most beautiful in terms of typography alone, without any other ornament. All these principles were also eloquently conveyed in 'The Ideal Book', a lecture Morris gave to the Bibliographical Society in 1893.

The Kelmscott Press was set up in 1890 in a rented cottage at 16 Upper Mall, just a few doors away from Kelmscott House: the following year it moved to more spacious premises at no. 21. The aim of the Press was to revive the allied art crafts of type-designing, fine printing and book production, producing hand-printed limited editions on handmade paper. William Bowden and his son were employed as compositors.

The Kelmscott Press was not part of Morris and Co. It was Morris's own private enterprise, the intentions of which he outlined in 'A Note by William Morris on his Aims in Founding the Kelmscott Press', published in the year of his death. This his last venture in design and craftsmanship was something of a 'late baby', taking up a great deal of his time and attention in the last six years of his life, although he received invaluable assistance from Sidney Cockerell, who was appointed Secretary to the Press in July 1894, and wrote a valuable *Short History and Description of*

Left: Morris and his daughter May, with the staff of the Kelmscott Press

Right: A beautiful example of Morris's calligraphy and decorative illumination made for Georgiana Burne-Jones in 1872

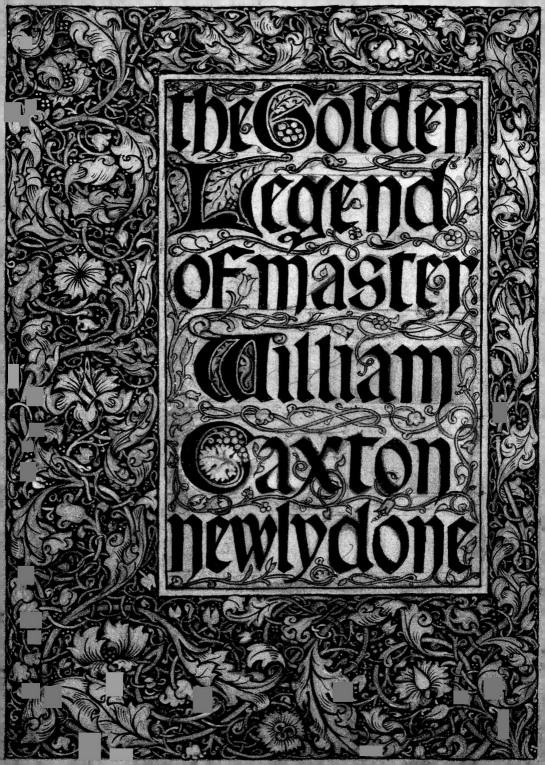

The Golden Legend of Master William Caxton newly done

the Kelmscott Press shortly after Morris's death.

The subsequent revival of small presses dedicated to fine hand-printing owed much to Morris's achievement with the Kelmscott Press. These included the Doves Press, started in 1899 by Emery Walker and Thomas Cobden-Sanderson; Charles Ricketts's Vale Press, C. R. Ashbee's Essex House Press, which employed some former Kelmscott Press staff; St John Hornby's Ashendene Press and Lucien Pissarro's Eragny Press. Morris had a far reaching effect on the work of American typographers, notably Theodore de Vinne and Bruce Rogers, and he is especially well represented in New York's Pierpont Morgan Library.

Morris's instinctive feeling for letter forms came from his intensive study of early manuscripts and printed books, and his inspiration for his type designs derived from the great 15th-century

Left: Original design by William Morris for the titlepage of The Golden Legend

Below: Morris's design for the Gothic typeface 'Troy'

printers, especially Jacobus Rubeus (Jacques le Rouge) and Nicolas Jenson. Morris's roman typeface, the 'Golden', was named after *The Golden Legend*, a popular collection of lives of the saints by the 13th-century Italian Jacobus de Voragine, which was translated into many languages. Caxton's English version, printed in 1483, was the model for the Kelmscott edition with which Morris planned to launch his list, although delays caused by problems in obtaining the right paper size prevented this (*The Golden Legend* became known at the Press as 'the interminable'). It was Morris's own *Story of the Glittering Plain*, in an edition of 200 copies and issued by Reeves and Turner, that was first off the press, in March 1891, followed by a selection of his verse, *Poems By the Way*.

Morris's own typefaces

Morris's Gothic typeface, the 'Troy', was named after another landmark by Caxton, his translation of the *Historyes of Troye*, the first book to be printed in England. Morris had planned to use 'Troy' for his monumental edition of Chaucer, but found that it was too big, so he designed a smaller variant of the 'Troy', the 'Chaucer'.

The Troy Type.

A B C D E F G H I J K L M N O P Q R S T U V W X Y Z

1 2 3 4 5 6 7 8 9 0

a b c d e f g h i j k l m n o p q r s t u v w x y z

æ œ & ff fi ffi fl ffl ! ? (' . , : ; - ,

The technique Morris adopted in the design of his typefaces is interesting. He did extensive research to find fine specimens of 15th-century type, which he then had photographically enlarged to enable him to study all their features closely. He was not using these photographs for copying purposes, but to help him find out for himself how the 15th-century craftsman tackled the intricacies of type design, and to discover the essence of the type, which he then modified in his own designs. Edward Prince cut the punches from which the matrices were struck by hand, and the type was then cast by the firm of Sir Charles Reed, under the personal supervision of Talbot Baines Reed, famous for his popular schoolboy stories, but also author of *A History of the Old English Letter Foundries* (1887).

The photographic enlargements which were crucial to Morris's type designing process were made by a printer friend, fellow socialist and neighbour at Hammersmith, Emery Walker. Although Walker was unable to accept Morris's invitation to join him in partnership at the Kelmscott Press, he undoubtedly played an important part in encouraging Morris's interest in fine printing through his own enthusiasm for it. Walker was a co-founder with Morris of the Arts and Crafts Exhibition Society and was persuaded – albeit somewhat reluctantly – to give a talk on printing as part of the lecture

Below: *The titlepage from the Kelmscott Chaucer, 1896, with the opening lines of 'The Prologue' to* The Canterbury Tales

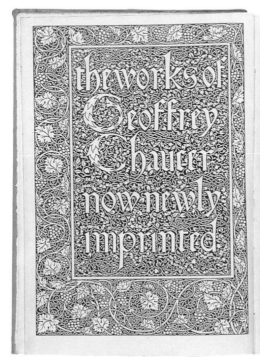

series accompanying the inaugural exhibition in November 1888. The lecture, which was a great success, was accompanied by lantern slides showing enlargements of examples of early typefaces, many provided by Morris himself, and it was seeing these slides that gave Morris the idea of designing his own typefaces.

Morris also made over 600 designs for initials, borders, title pages, inscriptions and printers' marks, producing these almost continuously through the last six years of his life. Most of them were engraved on wood by W. H. Hooper, C. E. Keats and W. Spielmayer. C. M. Gere and Arthur Gaskin worked as illustrators, as well as Burne-Jones.

Printing at the Kelmscott Press was done on three Albion hand-printing presses (one bought specially in January 1895 to cope with the massive Chaucer project), virtually identical in design,

Above left: Gold on green binding design by Morris and Webb for The Story of the Volsungs and Niblungs

Above right: Working on the Albion printing press at the Kelmscott Press

though made of metal rather than wood, to those used by Caxton. The paper, made from pure linen rag, as opposed to cotton, by Batchelor and Son, of Little Chart, near Ashford, Kent, was modelled on 15th-century Bolognese paper. Morris trusted Joseph Batchelor implicitly, and the mill produced three stocks of paper for the Kelmscott Press, all well-sized to give a fairly hard finish, and each with a distinctive watermark designed by Morris, combining his 'WM' initials with the distinctive devices of a primrose, a perch with a sprig in its mouth, and an apple set on a two-leaved stem.

Geoffrey Chaucer

Kelmscott

Here taketh the makere of this book his leve.

NOw preye I to hem alle that herkne this litel tretys or rede, that if ther be any thyng in it that liketh hem, that therof they thanken oure Lord Jhesu Crist, of whom proceedeth al wit and al goodnesse. And if ther be any thyng that displese hem, I preye hem also that they arette it to the defaute of myn unkonnynge, and nat to my wyl, that wolde ful fayn have seyd bettre if I hadde had konnynge. for oure boke seith: Al that is writen is writen for oure doctrine, and that is myn entente. Wherfore I biseke yow mekely, for the mercy of God, that ye preye for me, that Crist have mercy on me & foryeve me my giltes; and namely, of my translaciouns and enditynges of worldly vanitees, the whiche I revoke in my retracciouns: as is The book of Troylus; The book also of Fame; The book of the Nynetene Ladies; The book of the Duchesse; The book of Seint Valentynes day of the Parlement of Briddes; The Tales of Caunterbury, thilke that

sownen into synne; The book of the Leoun; and many another book, if they were in my remembrance; and many a song, and many a leccherous lay; that Crist, for his grete mercy, foryeve me the synne. But of the translacioun of Boece de Consolacione, & otthere bookes of Legendes of Seintes, and omelies, and moralitee, & devocioun, that thanke I oure Lord Jhesu Crist and his blisful mooder, & alle the seintes of hevene; bisekynge hem that they from hennesforth, unto my lyves ende, sende me grace to biwayle my giltes, & to studie to the salvacioun of my soule: and graunte me grace of verray penitence, confessioun and satisfaccioun to doon in this present lyf; thurgh the benigne grace of hym that is kyng of kynges, and preest over alle preestes, that boghte us with the precious blood of his herte; so that I may been oon of hem at the day of doome that shulle be saved. Quicumque Patre et Spiritu Sancto vivit et regnat Deus per omnia secula. Amen.

Here is ended the book of the Tales of Caunterbury, compiled by Geffrey Chaucer, of whose soule Jhesu Crist have mercy. Amen.

AN A.B.C. OF GEOFFREY CHAUCER

Incipit carmen secundum ordinem literarum Alphabeti.

AND AL MERCIABLE QUENE,
To whom that al this world fleeth for socour,
To have relees of sinne, sorwe and tene,
Glorious virgine, of alle floures flour,
To thee I flee, confounded in errour!
Help and releve, thou mighty debonaire,
Have mercy on my perilous langour!
Venquisshed me hath my cruel adversaire.

BOUNTEE so fix hath in thyn herte his tente,
That wel I wot thou wolt my socour be,
Thou canst not warne him that, with good entente,
Axeth thyn help. Thyn herte is ay so free,
Thou art largesse of pleyn felicitee,
Haven of refut, of quiete and of reste.
Lo, how that theves seven chasen me!
Help, lady bright, er that my ship to-breste!

COMFORT is noon, but in yow, lady dere,
For lo, my sinne and my confusioun,
Which oughten not in thy presence appere,
Han take on me a grevous accioun
Of verrey right and desperacioun;
And, as by right, they mighten wel austene
That I were worthy my dampnacioun,
Nere mercy of yow, blisful hevene quene.

Various inks were tried and tested but no English ones found satisfactory, so that finally, despite some protests from the workforce at the Press, the ink was imported from Jaenecke of Hanover. The binding of the books, in half holland or white pigskin, was handled by the firm of J. and J. Leighton.

A total of 53 titles – 18,234 volumes – were printed by the Kelmscott Press. Reissues of early books included Caxton's *Reynard the Fox*, the *Order of Chivalry* and *Godefroy of Boloyne*, as well as the *Historyes of Troye*. There were also editions of Shakespeare's *Poems*, Spenser's *Shepheardes Calender*, and of other favourite poets, Coleridge, Keats and Shelley. The entire Kelmscott Press list bore the hallmarks of Morris's own literary tastes, as illustrated, for example, by a charming little series of 13th-century French prose romances, translated by Morris, with which he had first fallen in love at Oxford. Planned but unexecuted projects included a volume of border ballads, a selection of English lyric poetry, the complete works of Shakespeare, Malory's *Morte d'Arthur*, Froissart's *Chronicles* and Scott's novels – all, as already seen, personal favourites of Morris.

To begin with, the Kelmscott Press was involved in the printing only, and the publishing was handled by Quaritch as well as Reeves and Turner, and Ellis and Elvey. However, at the end of 1892, Morris decided to turn publisher as well, and from then on, with one or two exceptions, such as Tennyson's *Maud*, which was published by Macmillan, he published all the Kelmscott Press titles himself.

Of these the *magnum opus* and veritable *tour de force* was the Kelmscott *Chaucer*; this was planned as early as 1892 but took four years to complete: cutting Burne-Jones's illustration designs in wood raised problems, but these were solved by Emery Walker, who made photographic prints which were worked over and then re-photographed before cutting. Then there were further problems with discoloration after printing finally began in August 1894.

Poignantly, the first two finished copies of the *Chaucer* came through in June 1896, just a few months before Morris's death. The edition contained 87 woodcuts by Burne-Jones and a title-page, 14 borders, 18 frames and 26 large initials by Morris, and was bound in white pigskin with silver clasps by Cobden-Sanderson's Doves bindery. These first copies were presented to Morris and Burne-Jones – Morris's copy is now in Exeter College Library.

By now Morris was suffering from advancing kidney disease, and on 3 October he died. His tombstone in Kelmscott churchyard, where his remains lie with those of his wife and daughters, was designed to a traditional Cotswold design, by his old friend and colleague, Philip Webb. Moving in its simplicity, it is a fitting tribute to all that William Morris, craftsman designer *par excellence*, stood for.

Above left: *Morris's design for the* Kelmscott Chaucer *binding, 1895*

Below left: *Pages from the* Chaucer, *1896*

REFERENCE SECTION

COLLECTIONS
Many museums and galleries throughout the world contain examples of Morris's work. Those listed below are of especial interest.

William Morris Gallery, Lloyd Park, Forest Road, London E17 4PP.
Housed in Water House, the Morris family home from 1848–56, the collection illustrates the development of Morris's career.
Open Tuesday to Saturday 10–1, 2–5; first Sunday of month 10–12, 2–5.

Victoria and Albert Museum, London, SW7 2RL.
Near comprehensive collection of textiles. Also tapestries, embroideries and furniture, and the Green Dining Room (now the Morris Room).

Wightwick Manor, near Wolverhampton, West Midlands. (Tel: Wolverhampton (0902) 761108)

Standen, East Grinstead, West Sussex. (Tel: East Grinstead (0342) 323029)

These two houses now belong to the National Trust and are regularly opened to the public. Both have shops which stock books and other items relating to Morris.

Kelmscott Manor, nr. Lechlade, Gloucestershire.
Open occasionally. For details, apply to The Society of Antiquaries of London, Burlington House, Piccadilly, London W1V 0HS.

Kelmscott House, 26 Upper Mall, London W6 9TA.
Open from 2–5 p.m. every Thursday and Saturday, Kelmscott House is also the headquarters of the **William Morris Society**, which exists to make Morris's life, work and ideas as widely known as possible. To this end, it organizes lectures, visits and exhibitions and publishes a quarterly newsletter and a journal. Send s.a.e. to the Hon. Sec. for details of membership.

Arthur Sanderson & Sons Ltd., Berners Street, London W1P 3AD (01-636 7800)

When Morris & Co. closed in 1940, Sandersons purchased all the original wallpaper printing blocks. They print specially commissioned papers from a wide range of Morris's designs, and also offer a selection of screen- and machine-printed wallpapers as well as fabrics.

SELECTED BIBLIOGRAPHY
Blunt, Wilfred Scawen, 'Clouds', *Country Life*, 19 November 1904

Bradley, Ian, *William Morris and His World*, Thames and Hudson, 1978

Catalogue of the Morris Collection, William Morris Gallery, Walthamstow, 1958

Clark, Fiona, *William Morris: Wallpapers and Chintzes*, Academy Editions, 1973

Crow, Gerald, 'William Morris, Designer', *Studio* (special issue), 1934

Fairclough, Oliver and Leary, Emmeline, *Textiles by William Morris and Morris and Co., (1861–1940)*, Thames and Hudson, 1981

Floud, Peter, 'Dating Morris Patterns', *Architectural Review*, 126, July 1959, 14–20

'The Wallpaper Designs of William Morris', *Penrose Annual*, LIV, 1960

Grylls, Rosalie (Lady Mander), 'Wightwick Manor: a William Morris Period-piece', *Connoisseur*, January 1962

Lethaby, W. R., *Philip Webb and His Work*, Oxford University Press, 1935

Lindsey, Jack, *William Morris*, Constable, 1975

Mackail, J. W., *The Life of William Morris*, 2 vols., Longmans, Green and Co., 1899

May Morris (1862–1938), exhibition catalogue, William Morris Gallery, Walthamstow, 1989

Mitchell, Charles, 'William Morris at St James's Palace', *Architectural Review*, January 1947

Morris, May, *William Morris, Artist, Writer, Socialist*, 2 vols., Blackwell, 1936

Morris and Co., Fine Art Society Catalogue, 1979

Naylor, Gillian, *William Morris by Himself*, Macdonald, 1988

Needham, Paul (ed.), *William Morris and the Art of the Book*, Oxford University Press, 1976

Parry, Linda, *William Morris Textiles*, Weidenfeld and Nicolson, 1983

Peterson, William S. (ed.), *William Morris, The Ideal Book*, University of California Press, 1982

Vallance, Aymer, *William Morris, His Art, His Writings and His Public Life*, George Bell and Sons, 1897

Victoria and Albert Museum, *William Morris*, HMSO, 1958

Watkinson, Ray, *William Morris as Designer*, Studio Vista, 1967

White, Gleeson, '1 Palace Green', *Studio*, 15, October 1898

INDEX

Page numbers in *italic* refer to the illustrations

ACKNOWLEDGEMENTS

The publishers wish to thank the following photographers and organisations for their kind permission to reproduce their photographs:

Ashmolean Museum 29, 102b; Birmingham Museum & Art Gallery 10, 54, 88, 89, 103; Bodleian Library 38; Bridgeman Art Library 57/John Bethell 108/Fine-Lines, Warwickshire Fine Art 16/Victoria & Albert Museum 13, 15b, 21, 22, 66, 72; British Library 117; The Castle Howard Collection 49; Country Life 109; Hulton Deutsch Company 23; Sonia Halliday Photographs 14t, 56, 60; A F Kersting 44bl & br, 75, 76, 77t, 78; Andrew Lawson 32; Macdonald & Company Ltd 113b/Pierpont Morgan Library 119/T Richards 4 (by courtesy of the National Trust), 14b, (by courtesy of Mr & Mrs Hollamby) 35, 40, 46, Trustees of Kelmscott House Trust 36, 71/Trustees of the Victoria & Albert Museum 8, 15t, 95, 110, 116/William Morris Gallery 12, 26, 50, 59, 61, 69, 70bl & br, 73, 80, 84, 86, 90bl & br, 93, 120, 122b; National Portrait Gallery 6, 33, 44; National Trust 87, 113t; Fionn Reilly endpapers, 68, 94r & l; St Brides Printing Library 52, 55, 121r; Society of Antiquaries 2, 43, 88, 122t; Tate Gallery 30, 34; Thomas Photographs 24; Trustees of the Victoria & Albert Museum 62–3, 64, 65, 67r & l, 74, 81, 91, 100–1, 102t, 105, 111; Weidenfeld & Nicolson 101; Whitworth Art Gallery 96, 99r & l; William Morris Gallery 9, 11, 18, 19, 27, 28, 67, 77b, 83, 97, 106, 114, 118, 121 left.

Editor	Anne Crane
Art Director	Alyson Kyles
Design	The Image
Design Assistant	Sarah Pollock
Production	Susan Brown
Picture Research	Julia Pashley